7/99

MAR   1999

646.77
ARO   Arons, Katie

          Sexy at any size

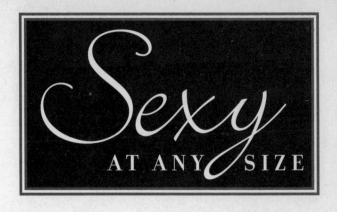

The Real Woman's Guide to Dating and Romance

Katie Arons

WITH JACQUELINE SHANNON

A FIRESIDE BOOK
PUBLISHED BY SIMON & SCHUSTER

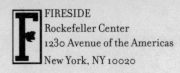

FIRESIDE
Rockefeller Center
1230 Avenue of the Americas
New York, NY 10020

FIRESIDE and colophon are registered trademarks
of Simon & Schuster Inc.

Designed by Diane Hobbing of Snap-Haus Graphics

Front cover: Photographer: Adriana Mejia
Makeup artist: Karina Del-Bel
Stylist: Samantha Weston
Model on left: Jack Phillips
Model on right: Phil Owens

Back cover: Photographer: Robert Whitman
Stylist: Liz Dillon
Dress courtesy of Onyx Nite

Manufactured in the United States of America

10 9 8 7 6 5 4 3 2 1

Library of Congress Cataloging-in-Publication Data

Arons, Katie.
    Sexy at any size : the real woman's guide to dating and romance / Katie
Arons with Jacqueline Shannon.
        p.   cm.
    "A Fireside book."
    Includes bibliographical references.
        1. Dating (Social customs)   2. Man-woman relationships.
    3. Overweight women—Psychology.   4. Body image in women.
    5. Beauty, Personal.   I. Shannon, Jacqueline.   II. Title.
    HQ801.A75   1999
    646.7'7—dc21   98-48293
                                                            CIP

ISBN 0-684-85415-5

ACKNOWLEDGMENTS

$\mathcal{M}$any thanks to my wonderful father and mother, Dick and Jo Arons, the world's greatest parents. Everything I am I am because of your love and support.

. . . $\mathcal{T}$o my big brothers, Scott, Rick, Tom, Paul, and Curt, who were always there to protect me, encourage me, and keep me in my place. To Marina, Luci, and Angel for becoming the sisters I never had. And to April and Adam, the next Arons generation.

. . . $\mathcal{T}$o the following people I call my special team of supporters. These are friends who believed in me, helped me, and wouldn't let me quit when I was down. Thank you all, Ricardo Alfonso, Dana Dillon, Peggy Lacayo, Janey Milstead, Martin Morgan, Martin Ryter, and Ann Whitney-Stubblefield.

$\mathcal{T}$hroughout my life, I crossed paths with many special people who touched me in unique ways to help inspire me during my journey. To all of these people, many of whom I will probably never meet again, I thank you.

$\mathcal{I}$ would like to thank the following for helping with this book and/or sharing their personal thoughts, stories, and advice: Emme Aronson, Lori Boyer, Liz Dillon, Mary Duffy, Dean Elston, Dr. Cheri Erdman, Kat Ferguson, Jackie Guerra, Wendy and Paul Johnsen, Natalie Laughlin, Eleni Savvaides, Catherine Schuller, Donald Siddall, Isabelle Tihanyi and Todd Wirths, Kelly Washington, Lora White, and Robert Witman.

Finally, thanks to my cowriter, Jacqueline, for understanding exactly what I wanted to say and translating it perfectly. And to my literary agent, Linda Konner. Thanks, Linda, for finding me and the idea. I wouldn't have written this if it hadn't been for you.

To all women who feel
bad about their bodies.
Life is too short, girls.
It's time to stop feeling bad and start living.

CONTENTS

I grew up hiding two major secrets. These secrets were the keys to my personality, and they controlled my every move. They are also responsible for why I decided to write this book.

The first secret: I was (and continue to be) absolutely boy crazy. Why was that a secret? Because—early on, at least—I found it worked better for me. My parents were both forty-something when I was born, and though I've always been close to my mom, we are from different generations, and boys and sex were subjects we didn't discuss much. As for my father, bless his heart, I think he believes that I am a thirty-two-year-old virgin. I am the youngest of six children—and the only girl—and all of my big brothers had friends. And since we lived right across the street from a park, and our house was always stocked with sodas, chips, and other goodies from my dad's restaurant supply business, our house in San Clemente, a southern California beach town, was *the* place to hang. I have been surrounded by men since the day I was born.

Ironically, though, that's what made me hide my boy craziness. It started with my first crush at the age of five. Paul was a teenager who lived across the street, and I thought he looked like Elvis Presley. I had a little record player and a 45 of "Love Me Tender." I used to play that record over and over, imagining that it was Paul singing the song to me. My brothers teased me mercilessly about this, and eventually one of them broke my 45. That was the last time I shared my feelings about boys with my brothers.

But my brothers weren't the only males whose behavior convinced me to stay mum. As I grew up, I saw what happened whenever a similarly boy-obsessed friend of mine (and I had several such friends) let a guy know she had a crush on him. He would make fun of her or, worse, avoid her completely. What I learned to do instead was to become pals with whomever I had a crush on and keep my fantasies about him to myself.

And I had plenty of other crushes in high school. Few knew the real reason I changed my class schedule so much—I wanted to be where the boys were! I even took Algebra 2 a year early—which meant I had to slog through both geometry and algebra at the same time—simply so I could get into a class with a lot of older guys.

And, boy, did I make my dad and my brothers—all of whom were jocks—happy when I signed on to take statistics at football and basketball games. I couldn't have cared less about the sports, but by doing stats I got to stand on the sidelines with the football players and ride the bus with the basketball team. Just me and the boys—the way I like it! I became buddies with dozens of guys, and I continue to have a lot of male friends today. These male friendships have given me a deep insight into what makes men tick, insight that I will share with you in this book.

But there was a flaw to my keep-your-fantasies-to-yourself strategy. Becoming buddies with a guy first, in hopes that the guy's interest in me would eventually turn romantic, didn't work any better than my friends' aggressive I-love-you-I-love-you-I-love-you-forever behavior. Sure, I became "one of the guys," but that's the way it stayed: I was one of the guys instead of WITH one of the guys.

I now know that often it's up to us to make our interest known. I'm not suggesting we revert to the panting "I've got a MAJOR crush on you" notes that never worked for my girlfriends in high school. I'm suggesting an intense but brief-as-a-spark come-hither look in your eyes or a touch on his arm that's just a split second longer than "friendly." In Chapter 5, "The Approach," I go into detail about why my new strategy works and how to pull it off.

I probably would have figured this out years ago—even in high school—but there was a big obstacle (literally) that crushed the kind of confidence a girl must have to go after a guy. And that obstacle was secret number two: I loathed myself because I was fat.

I have always been big. I was a chubby baby, the biggest girl in school, and I continue to weigh more than what society has deemed acceptable. I can't remember a time when I didn't think about my size, and some of my earliest memories have to do with people's reaction to it. The neighborhood kids could be cruel: "Katie, waity, two by four, couldn't fit through the bathroom door," they sang.

In my immediate family we have always survived by way of affectionate teasing, and very rarely did that teasing go somewhere that really hurt. Though my parents have always been big, my brothers were thin and I was the only child with a weight problem. I have no memories of my brothers ever really being cruel about my weight. Their teasing was more along the lines of "Katie's hungry again!" if I happened to point out a Dairy Queen when we were on the road. (Nowadays, I'm the only one in the family who does *not* battle weight gain.)

Other relatives, however, weren't always so gentle. My Great Aunt Chrissy, for example, used to constantly comment about what I ate or how much I weighed, and my gram would argue with her in my defense. Sometimes these arguments upset me so much that it almost hurt to breathe. And they left their mark on my developing sense of self.

One of my most painful experiences occurred in high school, after a couple of close friends and I got into a fight. I don't remember what the fight was about; what I do remember is the letter they wrote me when we were in the midst of it. It said something to the effect that I was disgusting because I was fat and that I had no self-respect since I was allowing myself to stay fat. These girls knew I battled my weight, they knew I tried diet after diet. They knew I cared about how I dressed, how tan I was . . . how I looked. How could they say I had no self-respect?

Through all of the years of teasing and mean remarks, I stayed strong on the outside. I always put on a happy face. I was outgoing and active. I didn't hide out. I rarely let people know how deeply they were hurting me. Instead, I'd go quietly to my room and cry, sobbing "Why me?" over and over again into my pillow.

My weight affected my every move. It was always my excuse. If a guy didn't like me, it was because I was big. If I didn't make a sports team or a play I'd tried out for, it was because I was big. If someone near me laughed, they were laughing at me because I was big.

Still, I kept up the strong front, and if you do that long enough you actually do become strong. It's that strength that has enabled me to travel the world and to get where I am today. But for years there was one thing I did not have the strength to battle, and that was the contempt I had for my own body. I starved it, subjected it to every fad diet that came along, took it to a variety of so-called weight-management experts, and even appealed on its behalf to the biggest expert of all: "Please, oh please, God," I used to say at the end of my nightly prayer, "please help me lose weight."

I don't do any of that anymore. Today, I am happy with who I am. I love my body just the way it is. I take care of myself and live my life. But the recovery of my self-esteem took years . . . and it started with just one sentence.

THE SENTENCE

In 1991 I had been modeling for a year and was living in Manhattan. My roommate at the time, Kelly Repassy, was one of the top plus-size models in the industry. She worked all the time and was always jaunting off to exotic locations for photo shoots. I was still considered a new model. And while I had managed to work a lot in Los Angeles and Miami and was now playing in the big league . . . , I wasn't working much at all. My self-esteem was at rock bottom because I'd been in the city for five months and not only was I broke, I was gaining weight. In those five months despite all my dieting efforts, and my lack of money, I'd still managed to grow from a size 16 to a size 18. I was miserable. This California beach girl wasn't cutting it in the Big Apple.

Then *BBW* came to town for a shoot. *BBW*, the magazine for big, beautiful women that has since suspended publication, was based in Los Angeles and had helped give me my start as a model. They booked me for a day of the shoot and booked my roommate for three days. I was excited because here was my chance to work with a model of her level. This was an important shoot for the magazine, so both the editor and the publication director were on the set. My self-esteem shrank even smaller: I felt like the proverbial small fish in a big pond.

It was during the lunch break in the studio of a famous photographer that I heard the sentence. The publication director, a stern, stocky woman with long black hair, leaned over to me and said, "You know, Katie, we love you at *BBW*.

You are one of the prettiest models we've ever used. But there is something in your eyes that says you don't like yourself. *Katie, you have a choice: You can either learn to accept yourself the way you are, or do something about it.*"

I had a choice! I did not *have* to be thin. No one had ever pointed that out to me before . . . and it had never occurred to me on my own.

I couldn't get her words out of my head. I'm a Libra—the scales, you know—and I tend to weigh out my options via "plus and minus" lists whenever I have a tough decision to make. That night I sat down and made the most important plus and minus list of my life. I wrote "size 14" on one piece of paper. That was the smallest I had ever been as an adult, and it had lasted only six months. I labeled another sheet of paper with my size at the time, the size I am to this day—size 18. Then I divided each paper into "positive" and "negative" columns and evaluated the most important aspects of my life—basically, men, health, activities, clothes, and career. I worked on these lists until I fell asleep.

The next morning, I got up and read over my work from the night before. It was an amazing thing, but the size 18 column listed one more positive than the size 14 column. I could maintain a size 18 with little effort; I could eat like a normal person. As a size 14, on the other hand, I would have to diet for the rest of my life. I would have to strictly limit my calories and work out five days a week. And even with all that effort, I would still be considered big by society's standards.

I spent the rest of that day walking around Manhattan. I strolled through Central Park, window shopped on the Upper West Side, braved the teeming sidewalks along Broadway and around Times Square. As I walked along in the city I'd hoped to conquer, I took a long hard look back at my crazy seesaw life as a dieter.

My mother had been a lifelong member of TOPS (Take Off Pounds Sensibly), and I had joined at the ripe old age of nine. In the TOPS program, you could diet any way you wanted to. I went on the Dr. Atkins diet, which was the most popular diet in the seventies. At that time, most people didn't know as much about nutrition as they do now. Members were counting either calories or carbohydrate grams, not fat grams. And no one ever talked about the importance of exercise. The Dr. Atkins diet was a high-protein, high-fat, no carbohydrate diet. You couldn't eat any fruits or vegetables, but you could eat unlimited amounts of food that didn't contain carbs, such as steak, pork, and cheese. The diet worked for me. That summer I lost twenty-three pounds and was named a state princess for the TOPS organization.

Before school started that year, my mother took me to the doctor for a checkup. He felt the Dr. Atkins diet was too extreme for a child my age, so he put me on thyroid medication and a low-calorie diet. He also recommended that we buy my first food scale. It wasn't long before I started gaining weight. I don't know if my body was reacting to the radical differences between the diets or if I was under-weighing my Puffed Rice. I just know that a new precedent was born: Once I started gaining weight on a diet, I would quit the diet.

Over the next few years, I tried Weight Watchers and the grapefruit diet, breaking out the old food scale on a daily basis. But I never seemed to lose any weight. The summer between seventh and eighth grades, I went back to the Dr. Atkins plan and again lost about twenty-five pounds eating cheese and pork rind nachos. That summer, I also grew three inches. I was feeling pretty good about myself. How well I remember the thrill of finally being able to wear a two-piece bathing suit and of shopping for an outfit at the hippest boutique in town. I now felt not only that I fit in, but that I had a good chance of becoming a part of the popular crowd at school. At my school, we called this cool group the "Soshies," and all of my carefully concealed crushes were on Soshie guys. I must have been pretty full of myself as I attempted to worm my way into that crowd, because my old non-Soshie friends didn't want to hang out with me anymore. The real blow, however, was that my weight loss didn't impress the Soshies—they were still too cool for me. My bubble really burst on one of the first days back at school when I got on the bus and one of the Soshie guys yelled to me, "Hey, Katie! You're looking pretty good. What do you have—just another fifteen pounds to go?" I look back at pictures of myself then and see that I was thin! The thinnest I'd be in my entire life! And yet that wasn't good enough. I slumped in my seat and felt like the fattest girl in the world.

The weight kept creeping back on. I couldn't tell you how much I weighed when I started high school because when I wasn't on a diet, I refused to get on a scale. I judged my body by the size number on the labels in my clothes. I was a size 14 as I entered high school. By the end of my sophomore year, I had ballooned up to a size 22. That's when I started my first liquid diet. Under a doctor's supervision—which included weekly blood tests—I ate no food, except for a protein powder that became a shake when it was mixed with ice and water in a blender, a soup when mixed with hot water, and a muffin when baked.

I lost more than thirty-five pounds in a couple of months . . . and then started cheating. At first, I would simply dab one of the regulation muffins with butter—"to vary the flavor," was my rationale. Then I ditched the muffins and put the butter on bread. Finally, I replaced the butter with peanut butter. The cheating caused me to feel immensely guilty, and with the guilt came bulimia. No one ever suspects a fat girl of being bulimic. After all, if you're throwing up food, how can you remain fat? The fact was that once I started cheating on the diet even the bulimia didn't help. I stopped losing weight. So I went off the protein powder diet.

Unfortunately, though, the bulimia stayed with me. My mother couldn't figure out where all of her food was going. A whole loaf of bread, for example, would disappear overnight. She suspected that my cousin, who was living with us while he went to college, was the culprit. I let him take the heat. I didn't confess until years later.

One of my friends was anorexic, and everybody knew it. When our parents were gone, we'd get together for bingeing sessions. We'd stuff our faces, then go to separate bathrooms to vomit, then come back for more food. It was a vicious cycle. During those days, I was more obsessed with food than I'd ever been in my life. When I binged I felt disgusted with myself—I was eating the way a *real* fat girl would. But then I would purge and feel better about myself. Purging was easy, *really* easy.

Nevertheless, the weight slowly crept back on, and the glory of purging wore off. It also became less of a private thing; soon, many of my friends knew what I was doing. What finally made me stop purging for good was a warning from a good friend. She told me about the health dangers, including the fact that purging eventually ruined one's teeth. My bright white smile had always been my favorite attribute—I didn't want to risk losing it. When I quit purging, I stopped bingeing as well.

I went back to eating normally, just like my friends. But the weight I'd lost on the protein powder diet came right back plus more and more. I had pretty much given up on the actuality of ever being thin, yet I continued to dream and pray. Occasionally, I made new efforts—such as trying Slim-Fast or visiting a hypnotist for help. I would lose a few pounds, but they would always come back—bringing a few of their friends along with them. By graduation, I was so big that we had to combine two graduation gowns to fit me. I walked up to get my diploma with an obvious foot of material added to the seams of the gown. I held my head high and smiled, but inside I was distraught. Though my tactful friends had assured me that they couldn't tell the gown had been altered, I was convinced everyone had noticed and was talking about it.

In my early adulthood I discovered that my weight varied as my lifestyle did. When I lived with five surfers in Hawaii, I lost weight. This was partially because I was following the guys' example: They ate healthily, they didn't eat much, and fast food wasn't easily available. Also, I earned my keep by running a "surfing taxi." I was the only person who had a car, so it was up to me to drive the guys to find the best surf breaks. This entailed hiking through cane fields to "secret spots" and spending the day playing in the ocean. In other words, I was active. In the four months I lived with the surfers, I shrank from a size 24 to a size 20 without dieting. I didn't even know I had lost the weight until one of the guys pointed it out to me.

The reverse happened when I returned to the mainland. I moved to San Diego to attend a travel agent school. I had no friends in San Diego—all I ever did was go to school and then come home to watch TV. I was so bored and miserable that soon the bulimia came back. Since I lived alone, it was easy to binge and purge. And once again, the weight returned.

I stayed big for the next few years. No matter what my lifestyle was, I didn't lose weight. In those years, I lived with the surfer guys again in Waikiki and did a lot of "adventure traveling" through the South Pacific, but I remained big.

Then came the day I saw an ad in the newspaper: "Are you fat?" it read. "It's not your fault." I called right away. That's how I met Dr. Lynch, an endocrinologist (a gland specialist) who explained to me that I was big not because of what I ate but because that's the way I was born. He said that on top of being genetically big, all my years of radical dieting—especially when I was still growing—had screwed up my system. My body didn't know how to react. Lynch's analogy was that my body didn't know the proper way to get its fuel to the engine. He got my system back in synch by prescribing amino acids and vitamins. My parents thought he was a wacko because he determined my needs with the aid of an allergy testing machine and kinetics. An example of the latter: He would have me push on my chest with one hand and he'd place a particular vitamin in the other hand. Then he would attempt to push the vitamin hand down. If he could do it, my body didn't need that particular vitamin. Sure, it sounds wacky, but this guy's methods worked for me. I lost more than twenty pounds without changing my lifestyle at all. And after he got my body chemistry in synch, diets started to work for me again.

That was right around the time the Optifast liquid diet was all the rage. Oprah Winfrey had just lost sixty pounds on it and had let the nation in on her secret. Today, both she and I know that a quick-weight-loss liquid diet is by no means the healthiest or safest way to lose weight. Like Oprah, most people who embark on such a program gain their weight back—and then some—once they return to eating regular food. But I had made the decision to change my life and my lifestyle. I made a commitment to myself to not only complete the Optifast program but to keep the weight off once I had finished it. In six months, I lost more than sixty-five pounds and got down to a size 14. I left the program only five pounds above my goal weight. And I maintained that weight, that size, for six months—those were the months I mentioned previously in which I was the thinnest I'd ever been as an adult.

Optifast benefited me in other ways, as well. It was a hospital-run program and I was assigned a personal trainer, who educated me about exercise and my strengths, and a nutritionist, who taught me all about food and how it affected my body. At one point, I was put underwater in a tank so that the team could determine how much of my weight was made up of fat. It was then that I learned that the smallest my body would ever be was just under 200 pounds—a far cry from those ideal height/weight charts that insurance companies publish.

But the most important thing that Optifast taught me was that I did, in fact, have willpower. Willpower! All of my life I was told that since I was fat, I had no willpower. If I had the will to be thin, why wasn't I? The Optifast experience convinced me that I was strong-willed, stronger than most. How many people can go without eating a bite of solid food for three months? Well, I did. I went through the Optifast program with fifteen other people. Half dropped out, and of the remaining half, I was the ONLY one who didn't cheat. Even Oprah had admitted to cheating on the program.

Soon after Optifast, I moved to Miami, simply to check out that part of the world. I got a job at the Park Central Hotel in Miami Beach, worked out regularly, and paid strict attention to what I was eating. Yet the pounds slowly crept back on. I was close to a size 16 when . . . I got discovered!

It was 1990, and Miami Beach was the hottest place in the country for fashion photography. Many of the photo teams stayed at the Park Central. I worked at the front desk and met many famous and important people. And I got the same backhanded praise I'd heard all my life: "You have such a pretty face. If only . . ."—you know the rest. Here I was, once again feeling thin but being told that I was not thin enough.

Then one day, Cory Bautista, one of the guys who had been paying me that sort of compliment, came to the front desk to tell me that he'd just been hired by Ford Models as an agent . . . and he wanted me to be a model.

I laughed. "You don't understand," I told him. "I can't get down to model size. I simply cannot get that thin."

Then *he* laughed and told me about the plus-size model market. "You can be a model," he said, "just the way you are!"

The memory of his words, plus "the sentence" from the BBW publication director and those lists I'd made the night ~~before~~ after are all responsible for the decision I made as I finally returned to my apartment on that autumn day in 1991. I was going to do what I had to do to learn to accept myself the way I was. And the first step? *I was never going to diet again.*

I'd like to tell you that I became the Queen of Self-Esteem that day. But let's be real. I had a lot of hard work in front of me. Suffice it to say that if you'd known that sullen non-New-Yorker-in-New-York of the early 1990s and then met up with me again in L.A. today, you'd be amazed. You'd be convinced that I'd undergone major attitude transplant surgery.

In fact, not too long ago, I ran into my "New York mom" and modeling mentor, the Ford Agency's Mary Duffy, for the first time in four years. We were attending a three-day Ms. Plus U.S.A. convention. Six times that weekend, Mary approached me, nodding her head with approval, and saying, "Katie, I like your new look. I like the woman you've grown into." I thanked her again and again, and the last time she said it, I told her, "I know who I am, I know where I'm going, and I'm doing it myself."

That attitude, I found, was a key factor in finding my sexiness and in revving up my love life. I learned about other vital ingredients, as well, and I'll share them throughout this book. But, first, let's hear why men are ready and willing to rev up *your* love life.

Among my five brothers, Rick has been my major source of brotherly advice over the years. For example, he once warned me that truckers and van drivers (of which he is one!) enjoy looking down at the women they pass in cars. "So make sure," he admonished me, "to keep your skirt pulled down over your legs." Well, yeah, that's good advice—except, of course, if the guy happens to be cute!

But Rick gave me another piece of advice that I now reject out of hand. When I was in junior high school and he was in his early twenties, he told me "Guys only get together with big girls because such girls are considered easy . . . desperate, in fact . . . and guys think they can get further with them."

Even after I started dating, a part of me believed what Rick said for years.

Being raised with brothers has often made me "one of the guys." I hear the way they talk to each other. One weekend a few years ago, when my parents went out of town, eight of my hometown buddies moved in. It was just me and the boys again, and it was nonstop fun and quite a bonding session (nothing kinky—all platonic). Let me tell you, these guys let it all out. They talked about *everything*—and listen to everything, I did. I didn't want to miss any inside information.

As a result of these heart-to-hearts with boys, all the traveling I've done, and my own self-acceptance steps (such as taking the initiative and approaching men, instead of just waiting for them to approach me), I threw caution to the wind and began to embrace another philosophy: MEN LIKE US! THEY REALLY DO!

As Kelly Bliss, M.Ed., wrote recently in her psychology Q & A column in *Dimensions* magazine: "Did you know that one of every twenty men prefers large women? Think of that the next time you walk into a room. If there are twenty men in there, statistically one of them will be drooling all over you!"

Well, thanks, Kelly, but I think you're being way too conservative with the numbers. Based on my experience, I'd say most men—especially more mature men—are looking for the whole package . . . not just a woman's body. They are looking for intelligence, a sense of humor, a love of life. As far as Kelly's statistics are concerned, I'd say it's one out of *ten* men who prefer a meatier woman. The problem is that half of those guys are just too embarrassed to "come out of the closet" about their preference in this weight-obsessed culture.

Backing me up is a wonderful book entitled *The Invisible Woman: Confronting Weight Prejudice in America* (for the specifics on this book and all others mentioned, see "Resources"). W. Charisse Goodman, author of *The Invisible Woman*, writes that once *BBW* began publishing in 1979, the magazine's Letters-to-the-Editor column was typically filled, month after month, with correspondence from big women who insisted they led happy, successful lives and were fed up with always being labeled miserable losers. "Are all these women, together with their boyfriends, lovers, husbands, and families, living a lie?" she writes. "Is each and every one of them suffering from delusions of grandeur?"

A more likely explanation, she says, is that our thin-obsessed society "is simply uncomfortable with men who will not submit to its strictures about whom they should or should not love and who are secure enough in their masculinity not to be intimidated by women who take up space."

Bonnie S. White, a writer who has spent years talking with big women and the men who love them, wholeheartedly agrees with that, and takes it further. In *BBW*, she wrote that being involved with a big woman "requires a certain amount of nonconformity on the part of the male. Some men just don't have this to give, and some men are in professions that make it even more difficult for them to act independently."

Perhaps that's why I've never dated the "suits"—salesmen, bankers, lawyers, and the like (yawn!). My gallery of past romances includes the far more freewheeling: the surfer, the biker dude, the barfly, the construction worker, the photographer, the model, the actor, the epitome of a rock star.

I'm not saying you're never going to find a nice attorney or accountant or financial planner to love you. But until society changes its attitude, he *will* have to possess at least a streak of ability to buck the status quo.

And how much do such courageous trendsetters like us? Let me count the ways.

THEY LOVE OUR PERSONALITIES
Men who answered a survey in *Mode* (a magazine for women size 12 and up) a couple of years ago said that a fuller-figured woman is more desirable than a thin woman

because (in order of importance): (1) She is more real, more honest; (2) She is less superficial; (3) She is less uptight; (4) She is more open-minded; and (5) She is more accessible and friendly.

Further, the surveyed men listed these personality traits as being superior in big women in comparison to thin women (again in order of importance): (1) femininity; (2) sensuality; (3) generosity; (4) warmth; and (5) self-confidence.

Now let's listen to a few individuals wax poetic (and not so poetic!) about our lovable selves:

Josh Max, writer, New York City: "To me, women of size are veritable canons of authority, sexuality, and power. When a big woman gets in touch with her inner dignity, attractiveness, and worth she is a force to be reckoned with. She is a walking example of the many years of work women have done establishing themselves at home and in the workplace based not upon what values others would foist upon them, but who they are as individuals."

J.D., law school student, San Francisco: "Big women have more love to give, and they're more sensual and intimate than thinner women. Whenever I step out with a big woman, I feel like I'm showing off a trophy. And that's especially true if the woman loves herself for being big. I don't care what a big woman wears, even if it's skin-tight and flashy. To me, that's just a sign that she loves herself, that she has confidence in herself."

Karl Edmund Morris, computer network manager, Abecon, New Jersey: "I love a BBW who is confident, openly self-assured, and cannot be contended with. She is fun to be around, smiles with the radiance of a summer sunflower, and commands attention like an ancient goddess in the present day. Physically, she is the epitome of feminine charm, beauty, and sexual maturity."

Randy Willis, writing in Belle *magazine:* "Since high school, full-figured women have always been in my life. Her soft-spoken manner and her confident attitude turn me on. It's what makes her stand out. A hefty honey isn't obsessed about her diet. She's not bowing to society's vision of what a 'beautiful' woman should be; her self-esteem is high."

(Note from Katie: See how many of these guys use words like "confidence" and "self-esteem"? If you need work in these areas, be sure to read the chapter called "How to Feel as Special as You Are.")

Kelly Washington, messenger and rap singer, New York City: "Big women have bigger hearts. They're more feminine, maternal, nurturing, and giving. And they're friendlier. When I approach one, I always get a response. That does *not* mean they're 'easier' to bed than thinner women. They aren't." (Touché, Brother Rick!)

By the way, most of the rap songs Kelly (known in rap as K. Foots) and his partner Donald Siddall (known as Ecstasy) write and perform all over New York extol their love of big women. They've graciously allowed me to reprint one verse here from their song "Bigger Is Better":

We've always liked 'em big and not small
Size 14 and up, whether short or tall.
It don't matter, no time to act shady
From head to toe, we love it all, baby.
Big and beautiful is good to go.
That's why we're up here to let you know.
Not to brag and boast to all of y'all
But to let you know we have love for all.
Big, beautiful, large, voluptuous women
You caught the eyes of us from the beginnin'
Not only physically and not only mentally

Fellas, hear me out and eventually
You'll comprehend why we did this gig
And why we support the big.
'Cause we're not about lies, it's the truth we bring
Yo fellas, y'all missing out on a good good thing!

THEY LOVE OUR FACES

Yes, yes, you and I have heard "But you have such a pretty face . . ." ad nauseam. But the guys you'll hear from next consider our pretty faces only part of the package:

Dean Elston, artist, San Clemente, California: "I love the innocence in the face of a bigger woman. It's somewhere between cherubic and childlike. There is something very precious about that face. I see more honesty and innocence in the face of a bigger woman than is ever evident in the face of even a stunning thin woman. The face of the bigger woman assures me that I won't be lied to or deceived. It's just so much easier for me to be close to a woman with that face." (Note from Katie: When Dean and I were in high school and those "No Fat Chicks" bumper stickers started to appear, Dean made "No Skinny Brains" bumper stickers to plaster over them!)

Nels Billsten, works for Boeing and is also pursuing an MBA at USC, Los Angeles: "Oftentimes, BBWs have beautiful faces—they don't have that drawn, stretched, malnourished look that you so often see in people who are taking great risks to remain thin. To me, the face of a bigger woman just looks heartier, and there's a fullness of health about it."

THEY LOVE US BECAUSE WE'LL EAT WITH THEM

Actress Jane Abbott (best known for her recurring role on *Evening Shade*, the sitcom that starred Burt Reynolds) said that she's always had a lot of men in her life, despite her size. "One thing I've noticed about men is that they like to have a woman who will eat with them," Jane says. "I've heard men say they hate to take out a woman, spend their money, and have her push her food around on her plate or just nibble. They know the woman is going to go home and eat."

My cowriter, Jacqueline Shannon, was asked to write an article for *Cosmo* on what bugs men most about women who are always dieting. She went into two San Diego offices to do interviews and was nearly tackled by guys, so desperate were they to voice their complaints. "I hate going to her house, scouting her freezer, and finding nothing but stacks of Lean Cuisine," one man said about his girlfriend. "If you wanna keep a man, that freezer should include at least a couple of Hungry Man pot pies."

Said another about his girlfriend: "It drives me crazy when she plays 'diet dictator' at a restaurant. She puts *everyone* at the table on a diet, by ordering the waiter not to bring us any chips and salsa."

Another gets miffed at his fiancée—and goes home hungry—when she invites him over for a home-cooked meal, then announces, "I'm just having broiled fish and some fresh carrots, but I'll make something extra for you." Says he, "That something extra always turns out to be a baked potato—without butter or sour cream, naturally. I usually have to stop for a couple of Big Macs on my way home."

Then there's the silent nagger. "My wife is always whipping out her fat gram counter," said one weary-looking male. "And I can tell she's secretly tallying up *my* grams as well. Makes me feel as desirable as Porky Pig."

The moral to these stories: Eat, eat, eat . . . and *enjoy* it.

THEY LOVE OUR SOFTNESS

Nels Billsten: "A warm and inviting BBW is a lot more appealing to me at the end of a hard day at the office than a boney, hard little woman. You just want to curl up with a BBW and relax."

Todd Wirths, scientist, San Diego (he lives with a bigger girl—my friend Izzy): "A lot of Izzy's friends are skinny, and when I hug them I can feel their shoulder blades, their backbones. They hit their sharp, boney chins on my shoulders. It's all kind of gross."

Josh Max: "When I moved in with my lady love, I was like a kid in a candy store for the first year. I could not keep my hands off her plump, soft, large, round body. I'd wake up in the middle of the night and stare at her lovely, curved, folded, dimpled form and wonder how I got so lucky."

Gilbert, actor and man of few words, Los Angeles: "Chunky but funky. More cushion for the pushin'. Fluffy and soft goes a long way. I once saw a magnet of a sheep on a refrigerator door and it read 'Ewes not fat—ewes fluffy.' My sentiments exactly."

THEY LOVE US BECAUSE WE'RE A PART OF THEIR CULTURE

You'll read far more about this in the chapter called "Where Blokes Love Big, Beautiful Women," but, for now, suffice it to say that in many cultures, big women are the *ideal*, not second best. In America, you'll find this expressed most by Hispanic and African-American men. As my San Diego buddy Izzy puts it, "Whenever I get waved at or blown a kiss from a car, the driver is always either Mexican or black." A New York City man who signed himself as "W.A." in a letter to *BBW* put it this way: "I'm probably guilty of being biased in favor of BBWs. It was a part of the culture (black) I grew up in. Being big or fat was less stigmatized. In fact, the phrase 'big, fine mama' was and is a positive affirmation of the concept that beauty comes in all sizes."

Rap artist Donald Siddall, a black New York City postal worker, told me that "Most of the people who brought me up were of size. That's the way I thought women were supposed to be."

But, wait. Lest you be tempted to conclude that men who love big women have some kind of unhealthy mother fixation, listen again to W. Charisse Goodman: ". . . If a man has been raised by a loving mother who just happens to be large, and he naturally associates largeness with love and therefore seeks that quality in a prospective mate, is that pathological?"

No way, she says, pointing out that millions of people—big, small, and in-between—seek mates who remind them of a parental figure.

"What is pathological," she concludes, "is the presumption that men who despise and automatically reject all large women simply have normal, healthy 'preferences,' but that any man who happens to appreciate big women . . . is disturbed."

THEY LOVE TO MAKE LOVE WITH US

In that same *Mode* survey I mentioned earlier, 43 percent of the men who responded said that fuller-figured women are better lovers in general (25 percent said thinner women; 32 percent "don't know"). The men who prefer bigger women said that what makes us better lovers is (1) We are less into ourselves; (2) We are more adventurous; (3) We are more romantic; and (4) We are less critical.

In my own interviews and research, I uncovered a myriad other reasons many men prefer to make love with a large woman. Lots of guys headed up their lists with just three words: "Big breasts . . . yes!" Another reason I often heard was that because we're big and strong, we're more like their "equals" in bed. Marcia Millman, an associate professor of sociology at the University of California at Santa Cruz, explains this well in her book *Such a Pretty Face*. She says such men find us more "durable" and less fragile than slender women. "With such a woman," she writes, "these men feel they can 'let themselves go' and have a kind of uninhibited sexual enjoyment that is not possible with a woman who is idealized and fragile."

My friend Dean Elston provided a graphic illustration of this when he told me about an "almost anorexic" woman he had dated: "Making love with her was one of the most uncomfortable intimate experiences I have ever had in my life. IT HURT! Those hipbones! She was so skinny I was afraid that if I hugged her . . . well, as Lenny put it in *Of Mice and Men*, 'I used to have a girlfriend, but she don't move no more.' I suppose most people would consider this woman stunning. But once she was out of her clothes, from my artist's point of view, everything about her physically was unattractive. It was just 'yuck.'"

Donald Siddall told me that sex is better with a bigger woman for "a million reasons." One of those reasons put a smile on my face: "I like working out and I like a challenge," Donald said. "While making love, I love the challenge of picking a big woman up!"

Let's hear last on this subject from Randy Willis, writing in *Belle* magazine: "Sexually, a full-figured woman is a gem, a treasure. She's a flower in full bloom, and she is never selfish. These qualities are true emanates of beauty and class."

So you go, girl!

See? There are lots of guys out there who have a preference for big women or simply don't care about body size. Then why are you still unattached?

If you're like me—or at least the way I used to be—you have probably written off every guy who wasn't attracted to you as being turned off by your size. It's a handy excuse to have around. We don't have to question why he didn't like us—we just *assume* we know. But what does a woman who doesn't have the weight excuse do when a man she's shown interest in doesn't respond in kind? She questions herself, thinks about how he read her, wonders what turned him off. She *analyzes* the circumstances. Well, we need to start analyzing, too.

That's why in this chapter we're going to throw out the size excuse and look at some other possibilities as to why we aren't getting the men we want. We will dissect the little things we do that are sending the wrong messages, and we will talk about ways to knock it off! The upcoming chapters "The Outer Shell" and "How to Feel as Special as You Are" will help you make major overhauls in the way you think about your body and in finding a style that will show off your body's assets. In this chapter, however, we're going to concentrate on what I believe are the primary mistakes in the way big women *act*, modes of operation that need to be fixed before *sharing your life with a man* can happen.

In researching this chapter, I questioned myself and had my friends do the same. We made in-depth observations of our fellow big women to determine what they—and we?—are doing wrong. As you read on I'm sure you will recognize these bad habits in women you know. We all have that friend who has simply given up on ever finding a guy and doesn't even try anymore. And we've all seen that big brassy chick at the bar who is making a bad name for all of us. In the next several pages, you may even recognize yourself. If that's the case, I can help you change your ways.

THE HIDER

When I lived in New York, I was friendly with two sisters. They were similar in many ways—they were in their late twenties, had their own apartments, worked long hours, were single, and both were big. Yet the sisters—let's call them Minnie and Maxie—differed in one major way. Maxie was always going out and about, catching movies, doing things with friends, sipping a drink at the local pub. She was rarely home because she was too busy living life. Minnie, on the other hand, had given up. She divided her time between work and her apartment. I'll never forget the first time I visited her at home. There was so much needlework I felt like I'd been transported to my grandma's house. Minnie obviously spent a lot of time crocheting blankets and embroidering pictures and pillows. She wasn't even thirty years old, and she was living the life of a sixty-five-year-old grandmother! If you'd met her, you'd have no idea that she lived like that. She looked and spoke her age. But her talk of men was always in the fantasy sense. She would share every detail of how her crush at work had exchanged a few words with her or had even deigned to smile as he walked past her desk.

Five years later, Maxie, the outgoing sister, is married. Minnie is still hiding and fantasizing. It's easy to get into the rut of hiding. It's a peaceful place, with no risks, no rejections. But it's lonely! Instead of going out and about the Hider spends her time elsewhere: at work, at home, on others, within herself. What has happened to Hiders like Minnie to make them give up? Minnie never told me, but Sandy, another Hider I know, had one date so disastrous and so hurtful that she is still hiding eight years later. Sandy had been set up on a double date with a man who was a friend of a male coworker. When the blind date saw her, his jaw dropped, and he ended up having a heated argument with Sandy's coworker . . . right in front of her! Sure, this kind of thing hurts like hell. But do you think it doesn't happen to skinny women? I have a slender friend who was once rejected because her butt was too small; another guy told her in no uncertain terms that her bachelor's degree wasn't enough for him. Since he had a Ph.D., this pompous ass feared she could not be his "intellectual equal." But she persisted and went on to find a real honey of a guy. So can you! As my dad says: "Different strokes for different folks."

If you're like Minnie and Sandy and spend most of your free time at home watching TV or doing arts and crafts projects, launch yourself on the road to recovery by taking this first simple step: Get out there and take extension classes. Or learn a participation sport. Says my friend Izzy: "I have a twin sister who's about a size 2. When we'd go to the beach, she'd get all of the attention from the guys. I figured I'd start surfing so I could hang with the boys!" Izzy's current boyfriend, Todd, is a great-looking geologist who Izzy taught to surf. Now they surf together. Surfing is a bit too much for most of us, but there are many other sports beloved by male prospects, such as tennis, golf, hiking, horseback riding, polo, and on and on. Bottom line: Get out of the house!

Regarding a different type of getting out of the house, many of us are struggling up that career ladder and the problem often is that we put our careers first and forget that a career is only a part of life. Or, as a wise truckdriver once put it to me, "A career ain't gonna keep you warm at night, babe." I'm not saying your career shouldn't be important to you, but you need to have more in your life than just what you do for a living. If you don't, you'll hit the top of the ladder only to discover that you don't have anyone to share the perks with! It doesn't have to be lonely at the top. If you're a workaholic it's time to reevaluate your schedule and figure out how to fit in some socializing.

When you're part of a large family as I am, there's always something happening that demands your time: refereeing a family feud, arranging a reunion, or dutifully devoting a day to Grandma. Other time-takers are friends constantly relying on you to solve their problems. I had a friend in high school who would call me in tears at two in the morning! She wanted me to hear every detail of her latest bout with her boyfriend and to reassure her that she was right. Pat yourself on the back for being a great friend/sister/daughter, but you can't always put others first. Learn to say no. One of my friends is a single mom with two kids and a full-time job. She has found this way of saying no very successful: "Say in a harried, semihysterical, somewhat breathless voice, 'Look, I wish I could help, but I can't. I'm simply overwhelmed.' I leave what I'm overwhelmed by to the caller's imagination, and I often add, 'Oh, God, there's the doorbell again. I've gotta go.'"

Experts advise that you ask yourself a handful of questions before saying yes to a request for your time: Do I *have* to do this? Is this project (or other person's problem) important to me? Do I have the energy and time for it? If your answer is no to any of these questions, then you should seriously consider making that your final answer. Yes, at first some of the time-stealers in your life are going to be pissed off, but eventually they will forgive you—and learn to love your new boyfriend!

The final type of Hider my friends and I have identified is the woman who *does* get out and about, but hides in her clothes. This is the woman who "tents" herself in baggy clothes and puts little effort into adorning herself. She walks with her head down and sits in the corner. This woman is hiding within herself. She knows that she has to be out there, but she doesn't really feel *worthy* of being out there. If you're like this, upcoming chapters are going to help you a lot. But, for now, remember my friend Eleni's mantra: "There's no such thing as an ugly woman, only a lazy one." She says, "Why would a man want to be with a woman who doesn't even make an effort—not just in her looks, but in her life?" Eleni's advice: "Hey, make an effort in life."

THE TOO MUCH

This woman is too pushy. She wears clothes that are too tight, too low cut. She looks cheap, slutty, and desperate . . . and she behaves that way, as well.

My friend Eleni says, "Big women who are too crass, too bold give big women in general a bad name. I went through a phase in my life when I did that. I did everything and anything I could to get a little more attention. It's a matter of craving attention because you're lacking it in your life. You are not getting what you need. You're not satisfied with the people in your life so you are doing something a little more outlandish so that people notice you." But this approach backfires: You may get attention, but it's not the kind you want.

Too Much girls are often too loud, too boisterous, too ribald. My friend Izzy remembers with a shudder the big woman she saw in a bar in Hawaii. "She had a guy on *her* lap and was totally wasted and obnoxious. I think that when you're a bigger woman you need to tone it down a little, because you're already getting more attention simply because you're bigger and are taking up more space."

Too Much girls often act like "one of the guys." Doing that was one of the biggest mistakes I used to make. I thought that if I got into "his" circle, he'd get to know me, fall in love with me, etc., etc. But that doesn't happen. If you're a buddy—especially a buddy with a mouth, as I was—you will remain a buddy. Izzy became "one of the guys" on her college surfing team. "Every year we had a semiformal dance—and not one of the guys on the team ever asked me to it," she says. "You're better off hanging with the girls." Izzy's boyfriend Todd says there's an easy way to determine if you've become "one of the guys": "If they fart in front of you, you're a buddy."

Another fault of mine that I've noticed in many of my big sisters is that we can be too bossy, too know-it-all. We get into the habit of doing for ourselves and helping others through their problems, so we are used to wearing the boss's hat. The problem with being a bossy woman is that *men* like to be the boss. You know how men won't stop and ask for directions when they're lost? It's that same mentality. Now I'm not suggesting that you turn into a sweet, subservient little mouse. But I do think that when you're trying to reel a guy in, you should keep your own bossiness in check and respect the guy's testosterone-driven need to prove he is manly or to at least have his own opinion!

I still have to make a concerted effort to keep my big

mouth shut. Believe me, this is one of the hardest things for me to do—but necessary. For instance, just last month, when I was with my brother Curt, we were talking to a San Clemente bar owner and I was giving him advice about getting local bands to play in order to bring in the local crowd. After I'd been stridently lecturing the guy for a few minutes, my brother interrupted with a sarcastic "Listen to Katie—she knows it all!" A total burn, but typical of my brothers. I know I had some good tips to give the bar owner, but I was going way overboard with my delivery. Curt put me in my place. If you don't have brothers in your life to do that, try observing other know-it-all women. You'll see how much of a turn-off that bossy bitch is, and it'll help you keep your own mouth shut.

Another way one can be Too Much is to be too pushy. You talk to men, but you don't let them respond. You get a guy's number and then call too soon and too much. You think you're trying to make it easy for him, but what you're really doing is scaring him away. You'll hear me say many times in this book that as big women we often have to be the aggressor, we have to make the first moves. But after those first moves, hold back a little and give him room to take the lead. I don't care how sexist it sounds—I know men well and I know that once you get the man, you have to let him lead, or you'll lose him.

THE SEEKER

The Seeker is the woman who is seeking more than she should from a man. She tries to validate herself through a man. You'll find this woman in all shapes and sizes—tall, short, slender, heavy. It's the goddess Hera in us (read more about goddesses in "How to Feel as Special as You Are"). The goddess Hera needs a man in her life in order to feel complete. But unlike Hera, many of us are looking for a man to fill needs that we really should be filling ourselves. Even Emme, a top plus-size model and author of *True Beauty*, was once a Seeker. She described to me her hesitation in accepting her love for Phillip, the man she eventually married. "For so many years," Emme says, "I was looking on the outside to find my femininity. I had to open up my mind not to judge Phillip on his size; to realize that since he wasn't a big guy and therefore would not make me feel feminine, I would have to get those feelings of femininity from within myself. I really had to buckle down and say, 'Hey, this is ridiculous. This guy is fantastic. He's wonderful! How can I even consider passing up this great opportunity to be with someone who is so awesome?' I had to decide that I was not going to make size an issue. It was interesting because it was a reversal of the way things usually are—he was not having a problem accepting me for my size, I was the one with the size acceptance problem."

We need to look within ourselves to find our strength, our power, our individuality, to become a whole and complete person.

THE THANKFUL

Many of us feel grateful when we get a guy. Let's stop that nonsense. We have to stop acting like someone is doing us a favor by being with us. There's nothing sexy about that. You have to walk around like you are the sexiest thing on the planet and that the guy by your side was not only lucky to meet you but lucky to get to spend some time with you, as well. Obviously, you don't have to say that out loud, but if you *act* that way—then you give off that vibe. Says comedian and actress Jackie Guerra: "As soon as I stopped acting grateful because a guy would smile at me or talk to me on a plane, I had my pick of guys!"

Jackie shares one of her other secrets: "The best advice

that anyone ever gave me was to treat myself the way I wanted the men in my life to treat me. As clichéd as it sounds, send yourself flowers, take long bubble baths, put on scented lotion, wear sexy lingerie whether or not there is a guy in your life. Because then you'll walk around knowing that you smell good and that you feel good. You *don't* walk around thinking, 'Oh, my God, he's not going to want me, and if he does he'll find out my elbows are rough!'"

Don't be the Hider, the Seeker, the Thankful, the Too Much. Be the Beloved. The rest of this book will show you how.

As I said at the beginning of the book, I did not become the Queen of Self-Esteem overnight after making the decision in New York City to never diet again. I had a lot of hard work ahead of me in what I call my "self-acceptance recovery." Even though I was modeling, I still wasn't comfortable calling myself a big, beautiful woman, and if friends saw me in magazines for heavy women, it just seemed to scream out, "Yes, folks, I am BIG!"

But I did make another radical, life-changing decision almost immediately: I moved back to southern California, determined to do things my way. If you're one of the eight million people who call the greater New York City area home, please understand that I love New York. But I can't live there. When I did, I felt like the proverbial fish out of water. The intensity of life in New York was absolutely Neptunian to a California beach girl, a happy-go-lucky round-the-world backpacker. The New York atmosphere drove me *nuts*.

I began spending every winter season modeling in Miami, fitting in a couple of trips a year to New York for jobs, but I spent most of my time modeling in L.A. No one else was doing that—I was told time and again that I'd never be able to make it without living in New York. But I did.

One of the biggest benefits was that I started working for L.A.–based *BBW* much more frequently. And one memorable day, I finally read *BBW*'s "statement of policy," which essentially is that big women are not alone and that we don't have to lose weight to achieve our goals. When I read those words, a lightbulb went off in my brain—no, let's make that a bolt of lightning. It made me think about the magazine in a whole new way, and from that day on, I read each issue from cover to cover. It was a huge step in my self-acceptance.

I spent a lot of time in the *BBW* offices and discovered a gold mine there—the magazine had an entire library of books about improving one's self-esteem. I'd read a lot of style and image books in the past to improve myself as a model, and these books always insisted that you needed self-esteem to improve your style and image. The problem? They didn't tell you how to get self-esteem. The books I found in the *BBW* library did, and I found myself reading them with all the page-turning rapture I had formerly reserved only for Anne Rice novels.

One book was particularly enlightening: Therapist Cheri K. Erdman's *Nothing to Lose: A Guide to Sane Living in a Larger Body*. With the backup of other researchers, Cheri dispels many myths and lies in this book, attacking, for example, the methods used to make up those "ideal height/weight" charts. She says that Louis Dublin, the biologist who developed the original charts for the Metropolitan Life Insurance Company back in the 1940s, used flawed statistics to come up with those figures. "The people used for the study," Cheri wrote, "were not representative of the population as a whole. The people whose weights were represented in the tables were a self-selected group who could afford to buy life insurance policies, which means that for the most part they were white, economically comfortable men, whose northern European ancestry favored tallness and leanness." Also, according to Cheri, there were no standard procedures for obtaining the study participants' weights, and many of the men underreported their weights. "Furthermore," she continues, "they reported their weights only once—when they purchased the [life insurance] policy. This meant that no data was gathered on weight fluctuations over the course of a lifetime." And—as we all know—we have a natural tendency to gain weight as we age.

I took another huge step toward self-love thanks to books like Erdman's . . . and not a moment too soon. At this point I'd already been on the cover of *BBW* three times, and I was beginning to make public appearances for the magazine. I didn't want to be a phony at these events; I didn't want to tell the heavy women I met that a woman can be big and beautiful without really believing it myself. But now I *did* believe it, and I made sure those women knew it. In return, they gave me another burst of self-esteem by looking up to me as a role model.

In fact, a bit of praise at one of those appearances gave me an idea of how to spread the big-can-be-beautiful message even farther. After I'd emceed a large-size fashion show at a mall, a woman came up to me and said her slightly plump twelve-year-old daughter had remarked with great excitement, "Did you hear what she said, Mom? I'm okay just the way I am!" That's when it hit me that I could really help young women, too. Not long after that I launched my newsletter, *Extra Hip*. The response to *Extra Hip* has been fantastic—especially after *Seventeen* magazine ran a small article about it. Goes to show you that there are a lot of frustrated and perhaps unhappy girls out there, just as there are among heavier adult women, who need to hear the message.

And that message is not only that you're all right just the way you are . . . but that you are *special*, as well.

FINDING—AND ACCEPTING—YOUR SPECIALNESS

We've all been dealt a hand in this life. The hand I was dealt includes my great family, my awesome parents, my intelligence, my drive, my willpower . . . and my big body.

You are a big woman, too. And no matter why you are a big woman—diet, genetics, etc.—the bottom line is this: There's a reason for it. It's one of the things we were meant to deal with in this life. We have been chosen, dammit!

No matter what I say, being big sucks in today's society. But now I actually thank God that He's given me this challenge to overcome—because overcoming it has made me better, stronger . . . special.

The first step in overcoming society's absurd prejudices and accepting yourself as special is to sit down, review your whole body history, and establish, once and for all, why you are big. You know what society thinks—you're big because you eat too much. But that's usually not the case—or, if it is, it's not the only factor. Ask yourself: What's the biggest I've ever been? The smallest? How big are my parents? My grandparents? What's my dieting history? Which diets have I tried? What happened after I stopped each of those diets? Are there lots of big women in my community or very few? Do I use food to relieve stress, anger, loneliness, depression? Do I really eat the exact same things as my thinner friends and continue to gain weight while they stay the same size?

If you can afford it, seek professional help in your quest to understand why you are the way you are. A psychologist can help you determine if your eating is tied to your emotions. Also, an endocrinologist can uncover whether your size has metabolic or hormonal origins. One of the best investments I ever made was with the Optifast diet program so that I could be weighed in an underwater weight tank. This method measures your lean weight against your fat weight. In simple terms, you learn the thinnest you can be while remaining healthy. I was stunned—and relieved—to hear that the *bottom* line for me is 185 pounds! (I feel comfortable at even twenty or thirty pounds over that weight, but don't get me wrong: I *still* can't just let myself go completely. I *do* have to watch what I eat and exercise regularly to maintain the weight at which I am comfortable.)

In reviewing my history, it also became quite clear to me that the size I am now has been primarily determined by three factors:

• Genetics. If both of your parents are big, as mine are, you have an 80 percent chance of being big yourself.

• An unnatural relationship with food. Because of my family's well-intentioned but misguided attempts to control my weight, I was often refused tasty foods. So I developed a craving for them. Actually, any kind of food became a treat.

• Wacked-out fad dieting. This completely screwed up my metabolism. I fell victim to the dreaded yo-yo dieting syndrome: I'd lose weight, gain it all back—and then some—all the way up to a size 24, at one point.

Knowing these things—knowing that for the most part my size is not my fault—made me feel stronger. Discovering what has made you the way you are will empower you, too, even if you *can* control your size, even if you're big simply because you sit around all day watching TV and eating Ben & Jerry's straight from the carton. Because once you know what you're all about, you either deal with it—you stop eating all that ice cream, or you get medication for that underactive thyroid—or you simply accept the fact that *this is it*. This is *you*. You stop asking "Why me?" You stop feeling guilty. And then you do everything you can to make yourself feel better about the unique and special hand you've been dealt. The rest of this chapter is devoted to the ways you can accomplish this.

Take heart in the fact that society's views of what constitutes female beauty are—slowly—changing

It was getting absurd there for a while in the late eighties—early nineties. Not only were women expected to be thin but well-toned and very busty, as well. I assure you, this combination occurs very rarely in nature.

There's a slow but steady backlash going on. Mostly because society is worried about its kids. People are finally getting alarmed by reports like these:

- A researcher asked fifth-graders how they rated in appearance compared to other boys and girls in their classes. A *dismaying 75 percent of the girls thought they were the least attractive girl in their class!*
- In another survey of fifth- and sixth-graders, *73 percent of the girls wished they were thinner, and 70 percent had already been on a diet.*

• One out of every four college-age women has an eating disorder.

The response, as *People* magazine characterized it in a cover story celebrating celebrities of size, was that "in every venue from films to fashion, stick-thin standards are waif-ing bye-bye." Here's some evidence of the progress that's been made:

• In today's sitcoms, big women are no longer relegated to the "sidekick" role—such as Vivian Vance's Ethel Mertz—as they were in the past. Not only do actresses like Queen Latifah and Kirstie Alley play lead roles, they are portrayed as sexy and desirable. And look who's one of the most popular television personalities of the decade: Rosie O'Donnell, size 18, who has vowed that there'll be no discussions of weight on her show. "Girls have such struggles with their body image, and I don't want to add to it," she told a reporter in 1997.

• We can now buy our daughters a "reality" paper doll—that is, a sweet, friendly looking, and pleasingly plump girl whom artist Leandra Spangler based on the Venus of Willendorf statue, which represented beauty in ancient times. The doll comes complete with enough outfits to take her to the beach or out on the town. And Mattel has announced plans to make a Barbie that better reflects real women—smaller boobs and a bigger waist and hips. Comedian Sinbad, who presides over the late-night show *Vibe*, said that he was all for making Barbies with rounder figures. "Because it's not only reality," Sinbad said, "it is also what a lot of men prefer." (Incidentally, soon after the Mattel announcement was made, I saw a newspaper cartoon in which a little girl was presented with this new Barbie. "Oh, good!" the girl said. "Now the other Barbies will have someone to make fun of!" Oh, well . . .)

• Seventy percent of the teen readers surveyed by *React* magazine said that singer Fiona Apple "looks like she needs a good meal."

• The most-envied woman of 1997–98 was Kate Winslet, who played Rose opposite Leonardo Di-Caprio's Jack in the smash hit *Titanic* . . . and she's no waif. The media's sniping about her weight was disgusting. As *W*, the fashion rag, put it, "[At the Golden Globe Awards,] Kate Winslet . . . sank any hopes she may have had of becoming a fashion icon by squeezing herself into a nude and black lace Pamela Dennis gown that barely stretched across her titanic girth." I guess the millions of guys who have fallen in love with her—just as women are swooning over Leo—don't count, huh? Let's applaud Kate for her response to this waspish media crap. Says she, "Some people are naturally very slim. I'm naturally curvy. I feel my responsibility as a successful English actress is to say to all those young women who are out there in turmoil about their weight—'Life is short, and it's here to be lived.'" Amen, Kate. Amen.

• Kellogg's Special K, MasterCard, Volkswagen, and American Airlines have begun advertising campaigns free of thin, shapely supermodels. According to Tom Dougherty, president of MR&O Advertising and Design in Philadelphia, these ads are still very much the exception to the rule. Still, it's a start.

• Even former fitness guru Jane "Feel the Burn" Fonda now admits she had eating disorders and got destructively compulsive about exercising. "Exercise," she recently advised in *Good Housekeeping*, "but don't freak out about being skinny. Some people will always be *round*. And there will always be men who like *round* women."

Do a reality check

Society does not live up to its own expectations. In other words, you are not alone. The average American woman is five foot four, weighs 147 pounds, and wears a size 14. Thirty-three percent of American women wear a size 16 or larger. There are as many women who wear size 18 as there are who wear size 8.

Check it out for yourself. Discreetly scrutinize a group of women in your own age group, in your everyday life, so that your idea of what real women look like becomes less dependent on the bodies you see in ads and on magazine covers. Do some "girl watching" at the beach or at the mall. A great place to do your own personal research is in a communal dressing room: Here in California, the legendary Nordstrom department store rigs one up for its semiannual sales. My cowriter, Jacqueline Shannon, says that when her daughter, Madeline, was four she got her own little consciousness raised in a Nordstrom's communal dressing room. Turning to Jacqueline wide-eyed as Jaqueline shrugged into a new suit, Madeline exclaimed, "Mommy, everybody's body is so *different!*" Jacqueline realized that, until then, "Barbie and I had been Madeline's only role models for what a partially naked adult woman's body looks like." (Just don't you stare at the women in the dressing rooms the way Madeline did or shout, "Mommy, some ladies' boobies are as little as mine!")

Realize that much of the "beauty" you see on television and in magazines is not natural. Many actresses and models resort to starvation and/or extreme exercise regimens (actress Julianne Phillips, for example, of TV's late *Sisters*, once disclosed that she did *6,000 abdominal crunches a week!*), and/or their beauty has been created surgically or photographically. No one knows about the latter better than I, a model. I wish every woman in the United States could watch a photographer's studio session with a model, just to witness the miracles the photographer can perform with lighting, lenses, and filters. And should a flaw somehow slip through onto film, there's a second line of defense ready and waiting: photo retouchers. The stars you see on the covers of women's magazines always get it in writing that retouching will be performed to their satisfaction. Furthermore, photographs of models are often trimmed with scissors, according to Naomi Wolf, author of *The Beauty Myth*. An alternative, she reports, is a computer graphics machine called Scitex, which alters just about every fashion or glamour photo that the public sees.

Savor praise
Start a list of every compliment you receive about your appearance. To restore your confidence, take this list out and read it over very slowly on days when you feel particularly insecure about your body.

The flip side to this suggestion: Stop negating expressions of praise from others, and you'll begin to stop negating them to yourself. When someone says "The color of that dress looks fantastic with your hair," don't say, "But it makes me look fat." Just say, "Thanks."

Make friends, or at least a truce, with your mirror
Spend five minutes a day standing nude in front of a mirror just looking at yourself. You'll start feeling more comfortable with your body as looking at it becomes routine.

Don't forget to admire the body parts you've always

liked. In her best-selling book *Revolution from Within: A Book of Self-Esteem*, Gloria Steinem said she's always been proud of the hands she inherited from her father. She went on to say that she makes a conscious effort to expand these positive, empowering feelings of approval to the rest of her body, as well.

You can do that. Contradict every negative opinion about your body that comes to mind. To revise an old maxim, "If you can't say something nice, then at least say something neutral." If you find yourself thinking, "My legs are so fat," and can't make yourself say, "My legs are beautiful," then go with, "My legs are strong."

Live in the now

"I always felt very ugly," comedian Jackie Guerra told me when I interviewed her for my newsletter *Extra Hip*. "It really caused me a lot of grief. That grief led to a nine-year battle with bulimia. I went through a period when I thought I was the most disgusting, horrendous person on the planet. But I'm so happy now!"

And how did that happen? She changed her attitude. "Often we get into a groove of thinking, 'Oh, I'll do that when I lose weight' or, 'If only I were thin I could be happy and beautiful' or, 'If only I looked like so-and-so.' Well, you know what? You just change it and you live right now."

Her advice is to first focus on yourself. Ask yourself these questions: Are you a good person? Are you healthy? Are you nice to people? Are you responsible? Are you compassionate? Do you have fun? Do you treat the people in your life well? Are you treated well?

Soon, says Jackie, you'll realize that the world seems much more tolerable, fun, and exciting.

Another way to live in the now: Get rid of all of those old

clothes in your closet that are too small and that you're saving for the day you lose weight. Those clothes are serving as nothing more than reproachful reminders. They are obstacles in learning to live in the now.

Body-acceptance therapist Cheri K. Erdman also recommends that you make a list of all the things you've always wanted to do but have been putting off until you lose weight. "Begin to take action on your list . . . NOW!" Erdman wrote in *BBW*. "Once you begin to accomplish those goals, you will have evidence that your weight is not in the way of having the life you want and deserve. You will learn that *you* have been in your way of having those things!"

Evaluate your best friends and other people you admire
Picture each person and ask yourself: What do I like best about him or her? It may surprise you to realize that looks are almost never at the top of the list. What we usually value most are features like "he's a great listener" or "she always makes me laugh." This exercise can help you understand that not only is your body size not everything, it often counts very little or not at all. Here's some scientific proof of that. A couple of years ago, *People* magazine teamed up with Marketing & Research Resources, Inc. of Frederick, Maryland, and conducted a body-image poll. One of their findings was that only 5 percent of women consider weight the principal characteristic in rating the attractiveness of others.

Have at least one "fat day" outfit
Every one of us has a dress or outfit that looks fabulous on us. It fits great, is in a favorite color, and always draws compliments. Wear it on days when you feel especially insecure about your body. Resist fashion if necessary

and concentrate on building a collection of such feel-good outfits so you can feel good about the way you look every day.

This is the favorite tactic of my friend and top plus-size model Natalie Laughlin when she wants to feel better about herself. "I choose things about myself that I find attractive or sexy, and when I dress I focus on that," she told me when I interviewed her for *Extra Hip*. "Like showing cleavage or my small waist. I sort of revel in my curviness; I find that more sexy than bone-thin straight. I like the fullness I see in me." A lot of other people do, too: Natalie's image has been posted on a fifty-foot billboard in New York City's Times Square for more than a year!

Look at photographs and paintings of women in earlier eras

Flip through old issues of *Life* magazine. See Marilyn Monroe, size 16, and her fellow voluptuites Jayne Mansfield and Jane Russell. Go to an art museum or check out art books from the library and seek out the paintings of Rembrandt, Renoir, Rubens, and Botero—all of whom glorified big women. This will show you just how much the definition of beauty changes over the years.

Cheri Erdman also recommends that you find a book about goddesses that includes illustrations or photographs of these usually zaftig legends. She suggests *The Once and Future Goddess* or *Goddesses and Heroines*. "Try to imagine your link to womanhood and femininity with these earlier images that represent creativity, prosperity, and abundance," Cheri writes in her book *Nothing to Lose*.

I take Cheri's advice one step further. Find the goddess in you. Here are some mythical goddesses with whom to link up and identify:

- **Artemis: Goddess of the hunt and the moon.** She personifies the independent, achievement-oriented feminine spirit.
- **Athena: Goddess of wisdom and craft.** She represents the logical, self-assured woman who is ruled by her head rather than her heart.
- **Hestia: Goddess of the hearth.** She embodies the patient and steady woman, who finds comfort in solitude and has lots of inner calm.
- **Hera: Goddess of marriage.** She has the essential goal of being married and making a commitment.
- **Demeter: Goddess of grain and the maternal archetype.** She represents a woman's motherly drive.
- **Persephone: Maiden and queen of the underworld.** She expresses passivity and the need to please.
- **Aphrodite: Goddess of love and beauty.** She impels women to fulfill creative and procreative functions.

Build up your self-esteem in other areas of your life

Studies have shown that as much as one-quarter of your self-esteem is made up of body image—that is, how positively or negatively you feel about it. However, psychologists also believe that the *most critical* ingredients to healthy self-esteem are (1) having a meaningful relationship and (2) having work you care about. If you succeed in one or both of these areas—and this book will help you find the first!—the confidence you engender can spill over and make you feel more confident about your body, too.

"I am a stay-at-home mom who weighs more than two hundred pounds," a woman once told my coauthor, "and I found that once I got involved in some extracurricular activities—I joined my church choir and became a Girl Scout leader—I not only had less time to dwell on my body, the fact that I'm fat also began to be crowded out by other factors when I think about who I am. I am no longer just a fat mother. I am also a woman who brings enjoyment to hundreds of people every Sunday morning and who is helping a dozen ten-year-old girls learn valuable life skills and serve their community."

Seek support
Again, I've been lucky. Working with other plus-size women, I've learned that I'm not alone. Listening to other women's personal stories has inspired me. You can get this benefit, too. Hang out with other bigger women. Start or join a support group. Or log onto an on-line support group, such as the Ample Living Forum on CompuServe. Read *Mode* and *Belle* magazines. Get more information on all of these alternatives in the "Resources" section.

Get professional help
If your poor body image has you mired in depression or is otherwise substantially interfering with your ability to live a normal life, seek professional help. A *cognitive* therapist, in particular, can help you change negative thought patterns. There are even therapists who specialize in treating women with body-image problems. You can find one by calling the eating disorders clinic at any major hospital and asking for a referral.

Read an enlightening book about body acceptance
Educate yourself. As part of the backlash against the impossible physical standards women are expected to adhere to, a slew of such books have been written in this decade. I've included a list of them in "Resources." These books

will help you learn how you came to hate your body and what you can do to change that.

Learn to identify the real triggers for negative feelings about your body

Psychologist Judith Rodin, author of *Body Traps: Breaking the Binds That Keep You from Feeling Good About Yourself*, which I highly recommend, suggests in her book that you sit down every night and note each time that you were critical of your body during the day. Then look for reasons you might have been angry at or disappointed in yourself at the time. Did you lose the courage to confront a coworker about not carrying her share of the workload? Did you have an argument with your sister? Dr. Rodin believes people often blame their bodies when external circumstances are really to blame. She feels that learning to identify what *really* triggered the negative feelings about your body can dissipate those negative feelings.

De-pain your painful feelings

In another highly recommended book, *Transforming Body Image: Learning to Love the Body You Have*, psychologist Marcia Germaine Hutchinson suggests that you draw a nude picture of yourself and circle the parts you don't like. Then write down exactly what you don't like about each part, such as "too big," "too much cellulite," or "too saggy." Hutchinson believes this drains some of the pain from such feelings, since repressed emotions have more power than those that are acknowledged.

I've given you a lot of good advice in this chapter from others. Now I want to finish by sharing what I call my self-esteem building blocks. I devised these a couple of years ago and keep them posted on the bulletin board next to my computer. In nutshells, they sum up a lot of what's been said in the previous pages, and give you a little extra food for thought, as well.

KATIE'S SELF-ESTEEM BUILDING BLOCKS

• **Get positive.** A negative attitude is very contagious. Find something positive about everything. Try to catch yourself being negative and change to a positive point of view.

• **Take care of your body and move on.** Realize that this is it—you look the way you do because it is the way you are meant to look. Take control: get rid of your scales; monitor where you feel uncomfortable and find new ways of doing similar things that give you a good sense of self rather than a bad sense of self.

• **Love.** Tell yourself, "I matter simply because I exist." Know that other people care for and love you. Love is like a trampoline that your self-esteem can bounce back on.

• **Connect.** Just like the spider web that needs many connections to hold it together in the wind, people need many connections. They give you a stronger foundation. Surround yourself with people who support you—not people who bring you down.

• **Find role models.** Think of real people who are already in your life whom you can admire; people who may not look beautiful but do beautiful things.

• **Empower yourself.** Assert your power by making decisions and taking risks.

• **Remember that you are worthwhile.** Know that "I can handle myself and my environment with confidence." Help others, try your best, and speak your mind.

• **Relish your uniqueness:** "I am the only me who ever was or ever will be." You are special—no one thinks like you.

Stop wanting to be like everybody else. See the things that you don't like about yourself and say, "YES! This has a place in ME!"

> *Look deep into yourself and think about*
> *who you are*
> *and*
> *where your self-worth is at.*

Back in my early days of modeling, I was hanging out in my tiny South Beach (Miami) apartment with a stylist friend of mine. A stylist is the person who dresses and accessorizes the models for fashion shoots. She was looking through my newly acquired fashion magazines when she launched into the life story of supermodel Christy Turlington.

"How come you know so much about her?" I asked.

"Oh, I've been reading this kind of magazine all my life," she replied.

"That's where we're different," I said. "I grew up reading *National Geographic* and *Surfer* magazine."

She seemed shocked. "Ah, small minds!" she said, with a tsk-tsk of the tongue.

She was serious. She felt her fashion interests were more important, more substantive than my own love for travel, beaches, and surfing.

While I certainly don't advocate our leading a shallow looks-oriented existence, I've learned that in order to be sexy, one must exude an air of confidence that is at least partially the result of feeling good about one's "outer shell." Therefore, I'm devoting this chapter to sharing all I've learned about fashion, hair, and makeup. But it's not just about confidence. I'm convinced that we're never going to correct people's misconceptions, their preconceived stereotypes about big people—such as that we're slovenly; that we let not just our weight go but everything else, too; that we don't care a whit about fashion; that we're dirty, smelly—until we all make a concerted effort to look our very best in public. And by public, I don't mean just at work or at the theater. I'm also talking about at the park and at the supermarket (terrific places to meet men, by the way). My operating philosophy is this: Any time a big woman walks out of her house, she represents me; and every time I walk out, I represent her. Read on.

It was hard to be fashionable when I was growing up because there was no fashion for fat little girls or big teenagers. I don't ever remember a time in my childhood when I had any choice about what outfit to buy. I had to get whatever fit. My basic uniform in high school was an elastic-waisted gauze skirt and a shirt with dolman sleeves, accessorized with seashell jewelry and the coolest flip-flops I could get my hands on. It was a look!

After high school, I pretty much stopped shopping because I traveled nonstop and lived out of a backpack. So you can imagine the looks of horror I encountered when I breezed into the Ford Modeling Agency in New York City wearing the same outfit I'd worn to the World Surfing Awards Banquet in Sydney, Australia, two years earlier. Interestingly, I had no idea there was anything wrong with my fashion sense. Frankly, I thought I looked pretty good.

A couple of things turned me around. First, the plus-size apparel industry exploded—finally! Eight years ago, there were only 200 plus-size clothing manufacturers. Today, there are more than 2,000 of them. And those manufacturers are finally listening to our pleas to give us well-made clothes that are fashionably in stride with anything in the misses department. As writer Sharon Greene Patton lamented in her book *Stop Dieting, Start Living*, most large-sized clothes used to be made of hideous polyester double knit, "as if," she wrote, "it had been decreed that natural fibers could not come in any size larger than a 12. In addition to being so shiny they could be seen in the dark, these clothes came in either sensible, dark colors, or shocking pink and lime green. There was no range of subtle, lovely colors and shades."

Well, times have certainly changed—to the point where popular designers like Anne Klein are offering large-size lines, and there are even couture fashion shows in Paris featuring only plus-size models.

My other wake-up call came when Ford sent me straight to Mary Duffy's house. Duffy is the grande dame of Ford's "Plus" division; she helps to groom new plus-size models, and she became my "New York mom." She took this stubborn, traveling beach bum and opened my mind to the world of style. She gave me my first of several books on how to maximize your good looks through fashion, including her own *H.O.A.X. FASHION FORMULA: Dress the Body Type You Have to Look Like the Body You Want*, which we'll talk about in a minute. Mary is famous for categorizing all women into four general style subsets: The "casuals" want to dress comfortably but tend to look sloppy; the "dramatics" stand out but have a habit of overaccessorizing; the "classics" want to look appropriate but often end up looking boring; and the "artistics" dress uniquely but can end up, as Mary puts it, looking "too, too, too."

My tutelage continued on the West Coast, where I was coached by the L.A. version of Mary. Linda Arroz was then the fashion editor of *BBW*, and she taught me to pay attention to the finer details of fashion: how different types of fabric lay on the body; how vertical lines achieve a slimming effect; why you should avoid horizontal breaks at the body's widest parts.

I went a little overboard when I first learned many of these rules. I was buying clothes that I didn't particularly like because I was so constrained by all of these rules. Then one day while shopping with one of my best friends, Dana, a fashion designer, things changed. I liked a pair of shoes but hesitated to buy them because they had ankle straps. "That's a no-no," I said to Dana. "Those ankle straps will make a horizontal break that will make my legs look shorter and stockier."

Dana couldn't stop laughing. "Those shoes make you look so sexy! Screw the rules!"

Dana is one of the most honest people I know. If those shoes hadn't looked good, she would have been the first to tell me. I bought them. That was the day I started bending the rules, and, as a result, developing my own personal style.

You can do that, too. I *am* going to give you some rules in this chapter. Just remember that they are not etched in stone. You simply need to know the rules in order to bend them! Also—keep in mind that different manufacturers use different "fit models"; that is, they base the cut of a garment on the body of the model who stands there draped in the fabric as the garment is designed. The result? One manufacturer's size 16 pants might be another manufacturer's size 20. So don't just grab something off the rack and head for the cash register. Always try it on first.

And . . . you must shop! I used to hate shopping with a passion because it was so depressing—clothes didn't fit or were just plain ugly. But, as I said, times have changed. When you head for the mall, drag along a shopping buddy to give you an honest appraisal of how something looks on you. You really can't trust salesclerks because they often (but not always) just want to make the sales. You can't trust mirrors, either. First, because they only reflect how we're feeling. And, second, we can't see ourselves the way others see us. We can't see the way an outfit is going to look from the back, or when we're walking, or when we're sitting down, or when the wind blows. But other people see us under those circumstances. If possible—if the dressing room isn't too dinky—try to do all those things. You'll have to fake the wind, of course.

IT'S A HOAX!

Let's get started with creating a personal style of your own. And that begins with the basics. Mary Duffy has graciously allowed me to share her H.O.A.X. system with you. This isn't her classification of style types. H.O.A.X. is based on the idea that bodies can be divided into four rough shapes—H, the straight-up-and-down figure; O, the round figure; A, the pear-shaped figure; and X, the hourglass-shaped figure—and that you should accentuate your positive figure features while playing down the negative ones. Keep in mind that not everyone is distinctly one figure type. I, for example, might be classified as "an X with an A rising." Also, your shape may change as you get older. My mom, for example, was an X for years. Now she says she's an "OHHHHHH!"

H IS THE LADDER-LIKE FIGURE

The straight-up-and-down body usually comes with a square or full-jawed oblong face. If you're an H, you're probably somewhat short-necked and small-busted. You don't have a clearly defined waist and your legs are slim or average. Your best features are hips, thighs, bust, and legs, and what you're aiming for, fashionwise, is the projection of a proportioned instead of straight body. While this is a wonderfully easy body type to dress, many H women have a negative self-image because they lack feminine curves.

The most flattering lines for an H create the illusion of a

smaller midsection (so opt for elasticized belts), or you can distract from it (hip wraps are for you). They emphasize thighs, lower hips, and legs (you'll look great in long sweaters) and cover the back of the neck (choose a portrait neckline). Body briefers, loose sweaters, and camisoles will also minimize that broad, fleshy back. Coat dresses, long necklaces, and V-necks will give you the illusion of a vertical line.

O IS FOR OVAL

The round, or oval-torso, figure is one of the hardest body types to dress. The O figure gives the appearance of round-ness. You probably have a rounded or oblong face with fleshy cheeks, a medium or large bust (making you some-what top heavy), a broad, somewhat fleshy back, and little or no waist definition with a tendency for midriff bulge. Below the waist, the O profile slims out with relatively slender legs (the O's greatest asset) in proportion to the top half of the body. The O woman is often saddled with "cutesy" clothes when what she really wants to project is glamour and sophistication.

If you're an O, you need to draw the eyes away from the top-heavy part of your figure toward the thighs, legs, and face.

O's can give the illusion of an indented waist through elasticized belts and blousoned V-neck shirts. You can distract from your middle torso by wearing hip-banded blousy tops. Leggings and tunic sweaters are good invest-ments (as they *aren't* for the other figure types) because they draw the eyes to your slim legs and thighs. You can create the illusion of more height with long beads and monotone dressing—all black, all blue, all whatever. Non-clingy fabrics, body briefers, camisoles, and full slips can help to deemphasize a fleshy back or belly.

A IS THE PEAR SHAPE

This is the hip or thigh-heavy figure. Think of the silhouette of the letter A—narrow at the top and tending to be big-bottomed. Most A's have an oval or heart-shaped face with a nicely defined chin, a slender neck, a small or medium bust, and a small back. The A's waist is clearly indented and shorter in length than the other figure types, and flows into fuller, heavy hips and thighs.

If you're an A, you need to choose styles that are A-line or full-skirted (but avoid gathers or pleats at the waist) and bring the eye to the waistline and upper torso. Your worst bets are styles that draw attention to the hips, thighs, and legs. You can draw attention to your midriff and waist with belts, waistbands, and set-in waists. Go for styles that broaden the upper torso, that create the illusion of upper and lower torso balance. What helps: shoulder pads, light-colored tops, dark bottoms. By choosing control-top hose and panty girdles, you can emphasize your graceful back and neck while drawing emphasis away from your lower torso.

X IS THE HOURGLASS

The hourglass figure usually comes with an oval or round face with a well-defined chin and an average neck. You have a medium or large bust with lovely cleavage, which can sometimes make you appear top-heavy. Your back is medium and slightly fleshy, and your waist is well defined, small, and very well indented. Your hips are round and full as is your derriere and tummy, which are proportionate to your bust. Thighs, legs, and arms are soft and shapely and average in size. Because yours is a curvy figure, you can be somewhat difficult to dress. Simple lines and soft fabrics suit the X best. Don't emphasize your bust—emphasize your waist and midriff. Do this by wearing belts and torso wraps in darker colors in nonclingy fabrics. Softer dirndl skirts and two-piece sweater dressing are good for emphasizing the soft curviness of the hip. You can also define the balance of your upper and lower measurements by wearing jumpsuits.

FIGURE FLAWS—MORE DO'S AND DON'TS

IF YOU HAVE . . .
. . . SHORT LEGS
DON'T cut your leg length by wearing tiered, flounced, or bordered skirts. Avoid pants with cuffs or tricky horizontal seams. In fact, beware of horizontal lines anywhere on an outfit. Ban long sweaters, jackets, and tunics from your closet because they tend to elongate the torso and make the legs look shorter.

DO wear straight-leg pants with a jacket that ends at the hipbone or waist. If you are small-busted, a bolero jacket or vest is also flattering. Wear pumps—and avoid ankle straps—for a long-legged look.

. . . A SHORT WAIST
DON'T shorten your upper torso even further by wearing high-waisted styles or wide belts. Short sweaters and jackets are also wrong, because they emphasize tummy bulge.

DO wear waistless or low-waisted dresses, yoked skirts and pants. Chanel-style jackets, tunics, and long sweaters are also good choices. If you wear a belt, make sure it's thin and the same color as your outfit.

. . . A FULL BUST
DON'T add to the fullness with fussy details above the waist. Avoid ruffles, gathers, puffed sleeves, and wide lapels. Beware of boatneck and crew necklines that don't break up the look of that generous bust. And please: When

it comes to showing cleavage, remember you can have too much of a good thing (see Chapter 2). A five-inch cleavage can come off as slutty or as "I'm desperate for attention." They're boobs, not a *shelf*.

DO wear V-necks. This is the very best style for you. Jackets worn over pants or skirts are also effective, giving you a slender, streamlined look.

. . . DERRIERE OR TUMMY BULGE

DON'T wear a dress or skirt that's form-fitting. Very fitted clothes, such as straight skirts, short battle jackets, and tight chemises reveal too much.

DO wear blouson styling, wrap skirts, hip-length jackets, A-shaped dresses, and easy tunics. Pants and skirts with controlled fullness at the top are also excellent.

WHATEVER YOUR PROBLEM

DON'T wear that old mainstay of plus-sized clothes—dropped sleeves. They look absolutely frumpy. Avoid dolman sleeves, too. They're out of style, and they look like huge wings.

DO wear neat, squared-up shoulders. Shoulder pads, incidentally, are a great way to make a garment skim over and hide fat on your back.

THE BATHING SUIT BLUES

Don't you hate it when your size 6 friends panic in the spring in anticipation of showing how "fat" they are in a swimsuit? How are *you* supposed to feel at the prospect of baring it all?

Well, don't you panic, too. I'm a born and bred beach girl and I have many years of experience in dressing so that I'll feel comfortable and good about myself among the beach crowd. Here's how you can do it:

• **Pool-party pretty:** Wear a really cute one-piece bathing suit that doubles as a body suit. Top it with a flowing skirt or shorts. Either way, remember your assets. If you have good legs, flaunt 'em. Go short. Complete your look with a longer, button-front shirt. Come to the beach or pool with it tied up, then wear it loose over your suit after you swim.

• **A hike and swim day:** You'll look killer if you invest in a good pair of bike shorts. Pair them with a sports bra or wear them over your one-piece. Cover it all with a big windbreaker or T-shirt and you're set. And, hey: There's no law that says you can't swim in bike shorts.

• **Beach babe:** This is the perfect opportunity to get in on a hot fashion trend—board shorts! That is, wear guys' swim trunks over your one-piece. Too timid to hit the menswear department? Then try wearing a sarong as a skirt over your suit. Sarongs come in gorgeous tropical patterns and colors and are lightweight and dry fast, so that you don't need to bother with a towel. You can swim in your board shorts or wear your sarong right up to the water's edge, drop the garment, swim, then put it back on as soon as you emerge from the water, dripping wet.

Finally, keep in mind that you're not covering up. You're not hiding yourself or your assets. It's exterior decorating!

LINGERIE

They're not making the Wonderbra—that little contraption that can make ANYBODY look bosomy—in plus sizes yet, and maybe that's a blessing in disguise: My cowriter tried one on one day and says it made her lips turn blue!

And so what if you can't have a Wonderbra? Be thankful

you're a large woman now instead of twenty years ago when plus-sized lingerie consisted of huge, ugly, industrial-strength, cow-yoke bras and waistline-banded white cotton "bloomer"-type underpants that must have made even someone as sexy as Sophia Loren feel like a frump. Today, lots of manufacturers make lingerie for large ladies that is hot, hot, HOT and that comes in a rainbow of get-his-undivided-attention colors.

I wear sexy lingerie when there's not even the slightest possibility I'm going to have sex. You should, too. It'll make you feel like you're hiding a sexy little secret, and that'll add a gleam to your eye. And who knows who might be watching when you're unloading your shopping cart and a bit of black lace accidentally comes into view?

Now, I also happen to be a big believer in shapewear; that being the euphemistic new name for what our mothers called girdles. In fact, speaking of my mother, when I was growing up, she was always buying me girdles. As often as other mothers ask stuff like, "Did you do your home-work?" my mother would ask, "Are you wearing your gir-dle?" The kind she bought me absolutely sucked. The nylon would make my butt break out, and the thing was always riding up. But times—and girdles—have changed, and this is one area in which mother really did know best. It's amazing—when you're wearing one, clothes lay against your body so much better.

My personal favorite shapewear is Givenche Ultimate Body Smoother Tough Support Pantyhose. I never go on a model shoot without them. They practically eliminate my cellulite and even out my saddle bags, give me the bare minimum of inner thigh rash, and I don't have to deal with panty/shapewear lines. They're tough, they don't run, and they are made all the way up to a size E, which fit me.

If you haven't ever looked at shapewear, let me tell you, there's something to fix or minimize every figure flaw, from a too-thick waist to tummy bulge to thunder thighs. There are even lots of all-over body shapers. You don't have to guess what does what—the tags tell you what the mission is. The fabrics vary somewhat, and so does the amount of control—i.e., light control (why bother?), medium control, firm control.

I don't recommend, however, revealing your shapewear to a man you're about to get horizontal with. Understandably, most of this stuff doesn't exactly look like something that would, as they say in the Bible, "stir the loins." See "How to Make Love to a Man—Big Time" for how to wear shapewear on a date and then sneakily get rid of it.

SHOES!

As popular plus-size model Christine Alt (her sister is supermodel Carol Alt) once said to me, "Too many women act like their bodies end at their ankles. Remember that people see your feet, too!" We bigger girls should wear the trendiest, best shoes possible . . . because most of us can! This is one area in which we can shop anywhere, because we wear the same sizes as everybody else. Just be sure to pick shoes that are comfortable as well as stylish. We put lots of weight on our feet, so be nice to them. And don't go out with run-down heels. Yes, people notice such things; run-down heels give the impression that you don't care how you look.

KATIE'S BEST SHOPPING TIPS

1. Know what's in style by reading fashion magazines. *Belle* and *Mode* feature fashions made just for you. Nevertheless, don't think that "thin" magazine fashions can't be

adapted for your wardrobe. By the same token, window-shop at all of the stores in the mall, not just the ones with the clothes that fit you. Look at what's on the mannequins in the misses departments, then try to come up with reasonable facsimiles in the departments/stores where you can find clothes that fit.

Another way to key in to what's currently in style is to watch hot TV shows like *Friends* and *Melrose Place.* Pay particular attention to what Kathy Najimy wears on *Veronica's Closet.* She always looks FANTASTIC.

2. Hit the men's departments. There are some hot guys' styles out there that look better on us than on them—and often (sexist though it may be) their stuff is cheaper. I've already mentioned guys' board shorts. Also hot-looking: Wearing guys' pajama pants in public. They fit! They flatter! And they're not always flannel! (They come in cotton, velvet, and silk, too.)

3. Don't rule out *any* kind of store for fashion finds. Jackie Guerra, a large-sized stand-up comedian who not so long ago had her own sitcom, told me she's even bought things at children's stores. "You can find tiny, adorable T-shirts to wear under jackets," she says. "Nobody knows that they only come to your midriff!" By the same token, hit the expensive stores like Neiman Marcus, even if you consider them way out of your budget. Glance at what's available and then hit the sales racks—you'll be surprised at the bargains you'll find. Or shop their outlet stores. Saks and Nordstrom are popular ones in my part of the country.

4. Don't discount discount stores. When I was young, my mother had to drag me kicking and screaming into Kmart. Well, these days, this is not your mother's Kmart. The retail clothing industry has gotten so competitive that even formerly frumpy places like Kmart have had to get with it to survive. I'm proud to say that I own more than one piece from Kmart.

One of my favorite ad campaigns a few years ago was from Target. In glossy magazine ads, they'd pair an expensive, designer-brand skirt or pants with a $9.99 blouse from Target. And it always looked fine. In fact, it always looked *great*. I bet those ads brought in a lot of people who used to sniff at the very idea of stepping through Target's supermarket-style doors.

5. Buy by the piece. I often buy a flowing skirt from one store, a tank top from another, and a sheer, flowery, long-sleeved blouse to tie over it from a third. To maximize your options (and your money), be sure you can mix the pieces with other things in your existing wardrobe.

6. Visit thrift stores. It takes patience and a good eye, but you really can happen on some finds! Some of my favorite, most-complimented-on outfits came from thrift stores . . . and we're talking the Salvation Army kind of stores, not the funky vintage ones that dot the trendy neighborhoods of L.A.

7. Experiment. Try things on. Don't go by how the garment looks on a hanger. Often you'll be pleasantly surprised and stumble onto a whole new look for yourself.

HAIR

Your hair is a neon light. A lot of guys say it's the first thing they see when they look at a woman. I see too many large women with frizzy old perms; dirty, stringy hair; bad color jobs; or color that is very obviously growing out. I'm also frustrated by the number of big women I see with football-player-type necks and short hair. They look like they have no necks at all.

My favorite hairstylist, Philip B. of the Beverly Hills Hotel, backs me up on this. Philip, who also has an exclusive line of products available at high-end department stores like Barney's and Neiman Marcus, says, "It's all about balance. When you're a big woman it is really important that your hair is giving you proportion. If you weigh more than 200 pounds, the last thing you want to do is go with a chin-length bob. You will look out of balance. One key to balancing your look is length. All men love long hair. It's like a primal need to them. They like to play with long hair, run their fingers through it. The other key to balance for a plus-size woman is volume. Even if your hair is fine you can lightly layer it to give it more body. I'm not talking about Monica Lewinsky hair. I'm saying that you need some proportion there. You can't be a big lady and have hair stuck to your head. Hair should flow."

Get your hair trimmed regularly. Keep up with what's in style—hot TV shows are the best guide—then pick something that's complementary to your body shape and lifestyle. Most of all, find the right hairstylist. In the end, that's the key to sporting really great hair.

HAIRDRESSER KNOW-HOW

1. Find a stylist you like. Word of mouth is your best bet. Ask women whose hair you admire—even if they're strangers—who their stylists are. Then shop around.
2. Look at your hair. What do you like about it? Is it easy to care for, or does it require too much attention? What do you want to change? What would you like to keep? Be prepared to give all of this information to your stylist.
3. Schedule a consultation. A consultation should be free and take about ten minutes. This is your opportunity to scope out the stylist and salon. It's always a good idea to arrive with pictures showing cuts and styles you admire. Be

realistic and plan to work with what nature has given you instead of against it.

4. Ask questions and be assertive. If you're not sure what the stylist means, ask him/her to explain or show you with pictures. Most salons are stocked with dozens of hair-styling books. If your stylist suggests something you definitely don't want, speak up, or you'll be wearing a hat or hiding at home for the next six weeks or more.

5. Make an appointment. If the stylist seems like a good fit, schedule a cut. Avoid getting a new hairstyle just before an important occasion; give yourself a week to get used to a new cut.

6. See the same stylist regularly. The stylist will get to know your hair needs and give you more personal attention.

7. Tip. It's customary to tip a stylist 15 to 20 percent of the bill, and I've always disregarded that old rule that you don't have to tip the person if he/she owns the salon. A smaller tip should be given to any assistants who shampoo or blow dry your hair.

MAKEUP

The one gripe I have about the makeup of most large women is that they don't wear foundation, resulting in shine and blotchiness . . . an I-don't-care-about-myself look. Starting your makeup routine by applying a good foundation is comparable to the way an artist paints a canvas white first. It makes the subsequent colors applied more even and vibrant; it keeps the canvas from absorbing the colors. The same goes for foundation, which has the added benefits of evening out the skin tone and protecting the skin from sun and pollution. Seal your foundation with powder before applying blush, eye-shadows, etc.

Another thing to keep in mind: The most definitive points on the face are the lips and the eyebrows, and the eyebrows are usually more of a problem. Don't go too bushy—whether that's in style or not—but do make sure you *have* eyebrows. Mine are very short so to elongate, I use a small, flat, angled brush with light brown eyebrow powder. If I'm going to have a long day, I apply translucent powder over that, then repeat the eyebrow powder/translucent powder layering two more times (powder layers are a good way to seal in lipstick, as well).

When plucking your eyebrows, follow your natural arch. If you've never done it, have it done by a professional the first time. You want the maximum amount of space—keeping in mind your natural arch—between your eyes and your eyebrows, because this makes your eyes look bigger. For that reason, don't pluck hairs on the *top* of your eyebrows. This "lowers" them.

Another trick I've learned from makeup artists is to contour. Make a fish face (suck in your cheeks) and use a darker foundation or powder below your cheekbones. You can also contour under your jawline and chin to help disguise a double chin. Apply a darker color under your chin and jawline and blend well into your neck. Contouring can be tricky, because if you do too much it looks like you're dressing for Halloween. Practice a subtle touch and check it in various lighting.

MAKEUP MONEY SAVERS

• Take advantage of free makeovers. Most cosmetic counters in major department stores offer them, and it's a great way to learn new makeup techniques. I had my first at Bloomingdale's in New York, and, aside from the foundation info I've given you, I recommend that you go in for a makeover at least once a year to check out the newest colors and trends. Caveat: Look at the saleswoman's makeup before you sit down and offer your face to her. If her makeup is too heavy, tell her nicely that you want a more natural look. Also, be sure to ask if a purchase is required at the time of the makeover; if so, talk her into letting you return later to make your purchase decision so you can check the colors in better light and test for staying power. Finally, be sure your skin is clean and fresh before the makeover begins, just as you would before putting on your makeup at home.

• If you don't have blotchiness and/or an uneven skin tone, you can opt for lighter coverage with a powder makeup instead of foundation. This way you get foundation and powder in one step, saving yourself time and money.

• Go for quality, not quantity, in your lipstick stock. Buy a few basic colors and layer to vary looks. Have one light or nude-colored lip liner for day and one dark lip liner for night. Own two or three basic shades of matte (nonshiny) lipstick that are right for your skin tone and that match or complement the primary colors of your wardrobe. A sheer frost lipstick or gloss can give any color a shimmer for a great change.

• You *can* get quality at a discount. Blushers, mascaras, and eye shadows are often made of the same ingredients—both drugstore and expensive department store brands are similar (what you're paying for is the packaging and the name). The off-the-shelf brands at drugstores can work just as well as the more expensive department stores brands. For example, many professional makeup artists swear that the German-made lip and eye pencils (one common brand is Prestige) available at drugstores are the best. Some makeup artists believe you can even find fantastic foundations at the drugstore. In a recent newspaper article, for example, a renowned makeup artist said that Revlon's Age-Defying foundation (around $8 or $9) is just as good as any foundation you'll find in a department store at three or more times the price. Many makeup artists also swear by Maybelline's Great Lash mascara (about $5), but I find it doesn't have the all-day staying power of some other inexpensive brands.

• Free gifts! Most cosmetic companies that sell products in department stores offer occasional gifts or "bonuses" with a minimum purchase, and often that's as little as $15. This is a great way to stock up on basics like mascara and lipstick, and you'll get some fun gift to boot. Just be sure the purchase you make really is an item that you need. Don't get lured into buying something just because it's bonus time (unless you really like what's in the bonus pack—then it's worth it!).

EXTRA TOUCHES THAT SHOW YOU CARE

Evelyn Roaman, one of the founders of the Roamans large-size clothing catalog, once wrote she always notices that overweight women almost universally have delicate, well-shaped, beautiful hands and feet. She says, "The plumpness that so distresses a size 8 woman is positively sought after when it comes to her hands. Plump hands are graceful hands; the skin is full and not coarse, and wrinkles affect a well-filled-out hand less than they do a thin, bony one."

Hands can also be a dead giveaway of one's true age. Even a beautiful, apparently youthful-looking woman's hands can be veiny, ropey, dry-looking, and covered with age spots. At any rate, make the most of your hands and feet. Wave your hands about when you're talking; wear bracelets and rings that will call attention to them; show off your nails with polish (see Best Nails Forward below). Most of all, keep them—in fact, keep ALL of you—smooth and supple. This is another way to prove 'em wrong, to prove that we do love ourselves enough to attend to our bodies. Here's how:

DO keep your skin clean. Perspiration left on the skin can damage the epidermis (top layer) of the skin and clog the pores, which will prevent the skin from breathing.

DON'T take long showers and baths. Hot water removes all the natural oils from the skin, leaving it excessively dry.

DON'T use harsh detergents and deodorant soaps. They can destroy the skin's protective layers, allowing the natural moisture to escape and leaving the skin rough and flaky.

DO exfoliate the skin, which aids in the shedding of dead skin. Use a pumice stone on the roughest areas of your body—the elbows and feet. (One of my quirks: Seeing someone with cracked heels literally can make me lose my lunch!) Employ a nubby washcloth everywhere else.

DO apply moisturizer right after bathing, after the skin is towel dried but still damp. This helps replenish lost oils and locks in moisture.

DON'T overexpose your skin to the sun. No matter what your skin type, you need sunblock, but avoid those that contain T10-2, an ingredient that leaves your skin dry and ashy.

DO drink gallons of water . . . well, at least eight glasses a day. I'm not going to go into all the health benefits of doing this—let me just stick with its effect on the skin. When I drink a lot of water, the lines on my forehead disappear. If you want more proof, just take a good look at your face in the mirror after you've come through a bout with the flu and are dehydrated. See how much more drawn and lined your skin looks?

BEST NAILS FORWARD

DON'T polish nails in the sun. The heat thickens the nail polish and makes it bubble.

DO keep nail polish in the refrigerator. This keeps it from thickening.

DON'T attempt to thin nail polish with polish remover. It dulls the finish. Use a product especially designed for thinning polish.

DO apply a clear base coat and top coat. The base coat protects your bare nails and prevents the yellow discoloration. The top coat is a sealer and keeps your polish looking shiny and fresh. It also prevents chipping.

DON'T peel off polish or pick at your nails—ever!

DO choose a soft, neutral, or sheer color for day and business wear. When in doubt, a French manicure is always appropriate.

DON'T let your nails grow out to Dragon Lady length. A sensible length lets you do things with your hands and has the added benefit of not grossing people out.

SCENTS

Speaking of grossing people out, I once nearly died of suffocation from holding my breath while a supersized makeup artist who smelled like a dirty belly button did my face for a photo shoot. If you're a big girl, you can't limit your cleansing and deodorizing routine just to your armpits. You need to tend to ALL of the creases on your body, including that major fault between your buttocks. I swear by powder (*perfumed* powder) and the well-endowed guys I know swear by the deodorizing effectiveness of powder, too. Mary Duffy, the fashion mentor I mentioned earlier in this chapter, recommends a different regimen: She says big women should apply deodorant to their hands then rub it in every crevice—especially the outer labia and inner thighs. According to Mary, this fix also protects against the inner thigh rash so many big women are prone to.

Oh, how I'd love to tell you that once you read this book and follow my advice you will be surrounded by men all fighting, fighting to win your attention. Even more, I'd love to tell you that I have never in my life had a hard time getting guys, or that now that I'm a self-assured, well-dressed model, I attract dozens of men every day and that I can get any guy I want. HA! The unfortunate truth is that I—and you—still have to work at getting a guy's attention.

In this chapter, we will discuss where to meet men as well as the various ways to catch the eye of prospective prey! We'll cover the basics from how to subtly flirt with him across a room, to how to carry yourself as you walk in his direction, to that ultimate goal: asking him out!

Some men will be easier prey than others. We live in a media-driven society, and just as we battle our physical shortcomings, men have pressure on them, too—to acquire a trophy woman. Just as we get the message that we're supposed to look like Pamela Anderson Lee, your average guy gets the message that having a hot babe who looks like Silicone Pam falling all over him will make him look like a stud.

Some of these guys are hopeless cases—they wouldn't be caught dead with a bigger woman. And I find that kind of a relief, you know? My skinny friends always seem to end up with guys who are obsessed with women's bodies. Who needs that? I think women obsess enough about their bodies as it is. We don't need any help, thank you very much.

Other guys genuinely like big women or have found themselves attracted to a bigger woman in the past but lack the *cojones* to do anything about it. As Nels Billsten, a male *BBW* reader, wrote to the magazine: "Growing up, I missed numerous opportunities to meet some wonderful women due to fears of what my friends and family would say. By the time I was 21, I decided to throw caution to the wind and began dating BBWs." In my experience, most men who admire big women have *not* reached the level that Nels has. But we can help them fight the battle against societal stigma. We're the strong ones in this situation. We've got experience in overcoming ignorant views about us. That confidence is one of the things that attracts men to us to begin with.

The first step in helping him overcome his insecurity is this: As a big woman, *nine times out of ten you'll have to make the first move.*

Another thing to always keep in mind: As the old saw goes, you can never judge a book by its cover. Men who love big women don't have a stereotypical look. Never assume a guy's preference based on the way he looks. At a big women's dance in New York City, I saw everything from conservatively dressed banker types to rappers to long-haired artists to guys who were wearing their delivery uniform shirts under their jackets. Every guy is prospective prey. It's just up to you to decide if he's got what you want. Does he spark your flame? Is he worthy of your admiration?

Read on and I'll show you how to tune in your approach-mode radar to weed out the wrong guys and help you pull in a winner. This radar, however, won't be 100 percent foolproof, if you'll pardon the pun. Should you happen to hit on a complete jerk or hopeless case, don't worry. In the next chapter we'll look at ways to handle rejection. But while we're on the subject of hopeless cases, let's start with a fuller discussion of them.

HOPELESS CASES

Women are open and emotional in their relationships with other women, but most guys play the game of macho. You'll never hear a guy telling his buddy how great he looks—they relate to each other in the same sort of sarcastically loving way in which I was raised. They may kid a guy about the way his girlfriend dresses or about her Hamburger Helper dinner parties. But joshing can turn nasty and outright cruel when the man is interested in one of us: a big woman. Some guys simply can't handle this. They lack the self-confidence and strength it takes to tell their friends how they honestly feel let alone to actually be seen with such a person. You'll know this type of guy because you'll catch him sneaking glances at you across the room, but when you do approach him, he nervously says something like "No, thanks" and turns away. Forget about him. Let him live in the shadows of what other people think. There are plenty of great guys who would be proud to be seen with you.

Then there are the guys who are just totally turned on by bones and would never be able to get hard for anything else. One of my closest friends is a sweet, Barbie-esque swimsuit model with a knockout body. Needless to say, she's always had a guy, but her stories of what these guys have said to her about her body freaked me out. One ex-boyfriend of hers once told her that she looked like she had gained three pounds and was getting soft, adding that she should work out extra hard that week. Three pounds! My weight varies three pounds from morning to night! I'd love to call this guy a dork, a narrow-minded pinhead—but I can't. That's his preference, just as we're the preference of other guys. Remember: "Different strokes for different folks."

Another boyfriend of Miss Barbie's used to tell her she was fat and that she should lose weight! A few years after they broke up, that guy started dating a bigger-butted friend of mine. He really liked the new girl and everything seemed fine. Nevertheless, I warned his new love about his past obsessive behavior. So she was well prepared when he eventually brought up the issue of her weight. She advised him that "This is it. Either get over it or split now." He got over it and never again uttered a word about her weight.

That just goes to show that people do change and that some seemingly hopeless cases can come around. But with all the great guys out there wanting to find a woman as great as you are, try not to waste your time waiting for a hopeless case to come around. Forget him and go find your knight in shining *amour*.

WHERE ARE THE KNIGHTS?
Boys, boys, boys—they are EVERYWHERE. Every single time you walk out your door, there's the possibility that you will meet your knight . . . or I should say *prince* since I'm a true believer that *all* girls are princesses. That's why it's so important to GET OUT! Unless you've got a thing for the mailman, you will not meet a man while you are at home. Think about it: The opportunities to meet men are as vast as the reasons you have to walk out the door. You never know who is going to be pumping his gas next to you, or standing behind you in the supermarket checkout line, or renting a video to watch alone, as you are. The possibilities are endless.

Help increase the odds by making sure that you are always feeling and looking put together every time you leave your house. Do keep in mind that there are certain times of day when it's better to run your errands because you increase your chances of meeting suitable single men. What kind of single man does his grocery shopping in the middle of a workday? Usually, an unemployed one! Most men are out there in the workforce, and if they are single the only opportunities they have to run their errands are before or after work. In my experience, not many guys shop on the weekend to stock up for the week. Men, by nature, have a "day-to-day" kind of mentality.

Supermarkets and Laundromats are swarming with men in the evening, around eight. These are hard-working guys who either worked late or went home from work for an hour or two before heading back out to do their errands.

Another interesting observation I've made is the number of babes who lurk about in public places in the morning hours. Yes, girls, it's the early chick who gets her worm. Try a coffee house. Most single guys don't bother to brew a pot of coffee before leaving for work; they stop to pick it up. Be there. It could become your regular coffee stop, too. Repeat run-ins are excellent opportunities.

My friend Lori Boyer, who is five feet tall and a size 20, often talks about her amazing success at meeting men while she's in her *car*. "It usually happens during rush hour," she says. "You're sitting in traffic, not moving, and you look over and notice there's a cute guy in the next car. You do the hair thing—if it's up, take it down, or just flip it over your shoulder—and then smile, *always* smile. Nine times out of ten they will smile back and often they'll ask you to pull over or for your phone number. If they approach my car, I roll down the window only about three inches. I never let anyone get in my car and I never give out my phone number. I usually tell a guy my first name. If he mentions sex right away, I'm outta there. But if he seems nice, I get his number or plan to meet him the next day. I often ask the guy why he stopped. Most of the time, he answers something like 'You have a beautiful smile' or 'You seem so friendly' or 'I've never had a girl smile at me in the car before.'"

Aside from the everyday rituals, like shopping for groceries or driving home from work through rush hour traffic, you should also make real efforts to get out to other places where you will meet single men. You can control your chances of meeting a guy who is right for you by picking a place that reflect your own interests. If you don't like to exercise, why look for a guy at a gym? If you're a dancing party girl, well, obviously you have to hit the club scene. If you like to read, cruise the bookstores and libraries. If you like to shop, try gender-neutral stores like Circuit City, Kmart, the Gap, and hardware stores, plus garage sales and flea markets. If you like sports, you've got an instant advantage: Sporting events are men smorgasbords! By all means, go to the games and go alone. Yes, I said *alone*.

GOING IT ALONE

Going out alone is a prospect that terrifies many of us. In high school, a friend commented that I never wanted to do anything alone, that I always had to have someone by my side. That made me feel kind of spineless, so I started to make an effort to go it alone, and years later I had built up the strength to travel the whole *world* alone. Sure, going solo does take some guts, but it's worth it. You have to be a little more careful and take some precautions—for example, I always try to valet park, and I'm always aware of what kind of people are around and who I talk to. But, generally, it's pretty safe out there. And there are some real benefits to being on your own. First, you can make your own judgments about who you want to meet, unclouded by your friends' opinions. It's also easier to approach a guy if you don't have a friend by your side, or a group of pals watching from a distance. Most importantly, you make it easier on the object of your desire, too. He'll be far more likely to approach you if he doesn't have to deal with the friend brigade.

MAKE AN ENTRANCE

Be positive and happy whenever you go out to meet new people. Who wants to talk to someone with a sourpuss face or a scaredy-cat presence? Also, how will you see them noticing you if you are staring at the floor? Be confident; keep in mind that you are worthy of being there and that any guy would be lucky to meet you.

Comedian and actress Jackie Guerra says, "When you walk into a room, walk in with the attitude that the people in the room are lucky because you have arrived, and they now have the great opportunity to get to know you."

My friend Dean Elston waxes eloquent on this subject when he talks about his girlfriend Eleni. "When Leni is there, to me she is the prettiest thing in the room. She's having more fun than anyone else. She's in the room picking out the fun parts about it, intensely enjoying the experience of whatever it is we're doing at that moment."

Confident women are women of higher quality, of higher status—they're sexier. Confident women are women men want to know.

TUNING IN

My friend Liz Dillon, who was the East Coast fashion editor of *BBW*, is always advising big women to be students of other women—to notice elegance and beauty, to notice women with a sense of joy that draws others near. What is radiating from that woman? Look around restaurants and clubs, says Liz, and you will see women who stand out, and they are not always the thinnest or the most beautiful.

I think you have to become a student of men, as well. Observe them carefully. What do you look at when you study your prospective prey? Just his looks? Well, look closer. Watch his behavior. Notice the way he dresses. Examine the friends he's with. By looking deeper, you can read a little more about the man before deciding if he's worth your attention.

We've all seen it, the group of arrogant studs who stand as judge and jury, making their opinions of every woman who walks by known to all. Now who wants that? Notice there's often a quiet guy in the group, one who actually looks ashamed to be with such jerks. He might have potential. On the other hand, what is he doing with such jerks to begin with? A man chooses his friends because they are like him . . . probably more than he's willing to admit.

Stay away from the guy who checks out every single woman in a tight dress. I had a hard time concealing my laughter one night as I watched one of them elbow his buddy every time he saw a babe. It was so childish. You just know that same guy calls his buddies after each date to give them the play-by-play lowdown on how far he got. Next!

My friend Susan always notices a man's shoes. She's an artist and loves going to see hardcore bands. She was going through a dry spell and caught herself dating a loser. "I should have known when he showed up for our first date wearing cowboy boots!" she says. As for me, even though I am a beach girl at heart, it still totally turns me off when a guy is wearing long pants and flip-flops. It makes me think that he doesn't own any closed-toe shoes. A man who has a fashion sense that you can relate to will probably have things to say that you'll relate to.

Look around the room for the guy who is happy, who is outgoing, who is also observant, and who seems confident and comfortable in his own skin. This is the type of guy who is approachable. He will be happy that you chose him. Or, at the very least, you'll have the potential to have a good conversation with him.

WALK THE WALK

Now we're ready to get into the actual approach.

The way a woman walks says a lot about who she is. Body language is how people read each other. It's the first signal we can control. Let's start with posture. Do not slouch. It not only makes you look bigger, it sends the message that you're insecure.

I found some terrific tips—all of which I've self-tested—from personal trainer Bob Shaw in an article called "Slimmer in a Snap" in *YM* magazine:

- Keep your shoulders back and lifted by squeezing the blades together.
- Center your head. Stretch it up toward the ceiling instead of letting it tilt to either side. (Or, as my mom always says, "Pretend there's a string holding your head up.")
- Contract your stomach muscles to help keep your spine up.
- Place your palms against your sides to keep your shoulders from hunching forward.

Next thing: Keep your feet straight when you walk. Big women tend to walk with their feet pointed outward. I caught myself getting into this habit because the staircase in my apartment building has narrow steps. I would run down them like a duck . . . and one day I caught myself going down steps on the runway that way! After I became aware of it, I stopped my duck waddle.

And don't stomp! Years ago I worked with a tiny woman who walked with such a thump that you could hear her coming from hallways away! Be graceful and delicate. As my friend Dean Elston says about his girlfriend, "Eleni is really a light angel. When she walks, she walks delicately. That is a presence."

Bottom line: Body language is everything. Straighten up your back and hike up those boobs and make sure that every aspect of your body is relaying what you would say in words . . . that you're sexy, special, and worth knowing.

THE DIRECT APPROACH

It takes confidence to actually make the first move, to make the approach and ask the BIG QUESTION: "Would you like to go out with me?" If you're like me and have suffered ridicule or criticism because of your appearance, then you know how bad it feels. If you can suffer that kind of humiliation, then why the hell can't you approach the guy and ask him out? You don't have to hit him with the big question right away. Often, I'll approach a guy with a neutral comment or question, my favorite being a simple "Hi!" Here's something my friend Todd suggests: "Ask him a question that will make him feel smart." My favorites: "Do you know what song this is?" or "Does this band have an album?" Then, the guy will either continue the conversation or move on, and you can predict this by either his response or his body language. We women are very good at intuiting when someone is attracted; researchers say it's because we're much better than men at seeing and interpreting nonverbal cues—such as how long a person holds eye contact. So come on, you can tell whether a guy is into you or not. If he's not, move on.

My friend Eleni's advice is to be direct. "Honesty—that is the only thing that has ever worked for me. I've always thought that honesty is the best policy. I was always direct. I would say, 'I think you're very attractive and I'd like to sit next to you and have a conversation over a drink, if you don't mind' and let it go from there."

Yes, you may get shot down. If you do, he wasn't the right guy for you. Don't let it bother you. Move on.

You can be direct without words, as well. One night a guy I had admired from afar for years joined my usual gang for a night out. He was giving me some attention but was not responding to my subtle flirtation. Finally, I decided to get a bit bolder, and as we sat across from each other in a bar booth, I put my feet up on the seat next to him. I said, "Oh, sorry. Do you mind?" I had his undivided attention from then on.

Men like direct women. It's another way of breaking the stereotype that big women are insecure or weak-willed. Many guys have told me stories of relationships where it was the woman's directness that turned them on.

My friend Todd, who is madly in love with a bigger woman, offers this advice about being direct: "Hit a guy in the arm—that'll get his attention. Just do something out of the ordinary. I was always flattered when a woman came up to me."

SECRET ENCOUNTERS

Here's another scenario: a man who likes you only when no one else is around. He doesn't take you out, but he loves to be with you alone in the dark. In most cases, this is a no-win situation for you. Women get more attached in their relationships, while men, on the other hand, often like the sex but remain emotionally unattached. Many of my friends have had their hearts broken by this kind of casual-sex relationship. They quietly let the guy get away with it and hope that he will change. Or they feel that having someone is better than no one. The problem with that is if you're spending your time with Mr. Closet, then you are not out there meeting Mr. Right. It's also very damaging to one's ego and confidence.

Sometimes the guy feels it's better to keep the relationship a secret until he's sure that there is a future with you. That's why honesty and patience play an important role when you are faced with the Secret Encounter. Ask him why he's not sharing you with the world and then decide if his excuse is worthy. If so, tell him you will put up with the charade for only . . . name your time—a month, six months, till Christmas, whatever.

I have friends of all types (big, small, unattractive, stunning) who have had secret romances. There's even a Certs commercial that depicts the typical scenario. A girl and a guy, seemingly strangers, do across-the-room flirting at a party. The girl leaves and the guy quickly follows. They meet in the elevator, and, as soon as the door closes, they kiss passionately and go home together. They are obviously an established couple playing a game. There is a secret thrill to the secret affair. Those across-the-room soulful gazes take on a whole new meaning. Just make sure that you know where you stand before you play the game.

WHAT IF YOU ALREADY KNOW HIM?

But what about guys you already know? Often there are guys in our own circle who get our blood boiling, but they're not making any moves. That doesn't mean: Give up, he's not interested. Maybe he's dealing with that insecurity we discussed earlier. Or maybe he's simply shy. Either way, you have to take action.

Is there someone at church, the office, the gym who

catches your eye, but you think he doesn't know you exist? Well, then go make sure he knows you! Take your time; patience can be the key when you're dealing with someone you see often. For starters, practice your across-the-room flirtation (check out Flirting Tips below). Then make a point of being near him. When you have a choice, choose to sit next to him. Arrange your schedule so that both of you tend to arrive at the same place at the same time. It may sound scheming, but it's really just a matter of being at the right place at the right time and taking advantage of an opportunity.

FLIRTING TIPS

Every relationship starts somewhere. The across-the-room flirtation is one important way. Here are some tips:

1. Smile. A smile says a lot! It says you are a happy and confident person. It says you are fun to be with and proud of who you are. Reread what my friend Lori says about smiling at guys in cars (page 90).

2. Catch his eye. My friends used to call me the "eagle eye" because I was always the first to spot a foxy guy. Then I would use that eye and reel him in. Watch a guy until he sees you looking at him, then give him a light, shy smile, and turn away. Wait a few minutes, and get caught again, this time holding his gaze just a bit longer. In your mind, say to yourself, "I like you, I like you." This will give your eyes the right look. And don't forget that smile. Here's the key: If the eye game is continuing and there is some interest, then you're ready to give *the question look*. Meet his gaze again and this time, instead of smiling, part your lips slightly and with your eyes, say, "Really? Me? You want me, don't you?" Often, this gets the guy off his perch and by your side within minutes.

3. Apply lipstick. I have had numerous men stare at me like hypnotized zombies when I reapply my lipstick. Here's the way my friend Lynn describes the process: "As you provocatively part your lips, you prepare to receive that ever-popular phallic symbol—the lipstick tube. He is reminded of petals opening in your loins. Let's not forget Georgia O'Keeffe's flower paintings and why they are considered so erotic. When people look at O'Keeffe paintings for a while, they see vaginal openings in the form of these beautiful flowers. The art of applying lipstick is surrounded by sexual symbolism."

4. Touch yourself. With your hands, feel your skin in a sensual way—around the throat, down your cleavage a bit. There are certain areas a woman can touch that send very erotic signals to the man who is watching.

5. Dance! Music can be the biggest aphrodisiac in the world. It not only makes you feel sexy, it makes any man watching you feel hot, too . . . hot for *you*. Let me back that up with a little story. Recently, I was out with one of my little "hotty" friends. This girl is blessed with The Package—great hair, body, and looks. She absolutely exudes sex appeal. We went to this trendy, snobby, Eurotrash L.A. bar. It wasn't very crowded, and no one could bother to look at us. Nor did anyone seem to speak English. The music, however, was super!

Finally, I just got out on the floor and started moving. I was the only one dancing. Yes, people stared at me, but I didn't care. I didn't know any of them and had no desire to.

My friend joined me, then a guy joined her. That was okay; I'm used to her getting attention from guys first. And those guys always turn out to be major losers. I just continued dancing . . . flowing, dipping, gliding on my own. When I stopped, a couple of guys who had completely ignored me earlier were all over me! "Sit by me!" each begged. Others came up to me later, intrigued: "Who are you? What do you do?"

If I'd let my insecurity win that night, I would have been bored to death and would have gone home blaming that snotty crowd for my misery. Instead, I had a great night filled with compliments, long, hard looks, and interesting offers (that I passed on, by the way!).

6. Practice flirting. Do it with a bartender. They are used to flirting. Girls are constantly hanging over the bar, waving their hands to get a drink. Try it. Lean over the bar, throw your chest out, stand on your toes, smile, wink. It's safe and acceptable to flirt with him, because he knows you just want his . . . drink!

In this chapter, we're going to deal with two kinds of rejection—the kind you may get if you make a move on a guy who turns out to not be interested, and the unsolicited kind you get from people who just have a problem with your size and think they have the right to let you know. Let's begin our discussion with the latter jerks first.

I used to want to be popular; I was devastated when someone didn't like me, or was mad at me, and let me know by making fun of my size. I tried to avoid confrontations—although in elementary school I was a pretty darn good fighter. And when I did fight, the kids looking on would always shout, "Sit on him, Katie! Sit on him!" I would fight even harder so I wouldn't have to resort to that (although one time, sitting on my tormentor was the only way to end the fight).

COPING WITH REJECTION

As I got older, I started handling rejection in one of three ways: I ignored it (a good choice); I simply smiled (not so good); or I answered a taunt with a joking, self-ridiculing remark (terrible!). An example of this: While walking on the beach as a teenager, I passed a twelve-year-old kid I knew who called out something about my huge boobs. In response, I said, "Yeah! They're just like a couple of water balloons, aren't they?"

I cringe at the memory. Because do you see what I was doing? By putting myself down I was letting that kid know that what he said was okay; I was justifying that little brat's rude behavior.

Similarly, in high school, when I was running for a class office, I wanted my campaign slogan to be "Vote for Katie and Get a Ton of Fun." Fortunately, before I made my posters, my parents convinced me that putting myself down would make me look like a weak candidate. (I changed my slogan and won the election. Thanks, Mom and Dad!) *Never* put yourself down!

The primary purpose of my self-ridicule was that I didn't want hecklers to know that they hurt me. I didn't want anyone to know that I cared what they thought. But of course I did. I cared desperately. But I wouldn't defend myself. Some of my friends would take on the task of defending me against jerks—"Hey, don't say that to her!" or, "Be quiet. That's not nice"—but I would never think of saying it for myself. In addition to my fear of being seen as wounded, I also feared that to fight back would just provoke my attacker even more.

In the last decade, however, I've discovered that it's just the opposite that's true. Depending on the circumstances, as well as the intentions and nastiness of the tormentor, when I now choose to stand up for myself I feel empowered. I've sent the jerk the message that it's not all right to make fun of somebody's size. And either because I've made him feel ashamed, or he didn't get the reaction he wanted, or I've embarrassed him in front of his buds, that heckler is much more likely to back off. What's more, he'll probably think twice before he insults someone again.

Now I must admit that a few years ago I did revert to one of my old childish ways. I was in a crowded bar talking to a friend when a guy behind me, trying to get to the bar, said "You're supposed to walk, not talk. Move it!" I said, "Go around me." And he responded "I can't get around your fat ass." What did I do? I whirled around and slugged the guy! I could see that he was about to slug me back, so I went into "poor little girl" mode. "Oh, my God, he's going to hit me!" I shouted. "Please don't hit me!" This drew everyone's attention—and the guy got tossed out of the bar as I called after him, "You're just a short guy with a big nose and a Napoleon complex!"

I don't recommend slugging unless you've grown up strong and a good slugger like me—thanks to fights with my brothers!

Seriously, the best ways to fight back are (1) ignore the ignoramus; (2) educate him; (3) tell him to shut up in a nice way; and (4) insult him right back.

IGNORE THE IGNORAMUS

This works particularly well when someone mutters something derogatory and you can legitimately pretend that you simply didn't hear him. When I'm modeling I have to use this tactic and keep my big mouth shut or risk losing a client. But it's difficult, let me tell you. I have to put up with comments on the set such as, "Oh, no! Not that angle! Her butt looks HUGE!" Once, when I was in an informal fashion show near a mall entrance, a passerby said, "Oh, look—there's a big one!" Boy, did I want to say something, *anything*, but I was being paid to be a mannequin, and mannequins don't talk.

By being forced to ignore put-downs I've felt the peaceful benefits of just letting it go. Sometimes, it's best to just forgive their simpleminded, lame-ass comments and forget that the people who said them ever existed.

EDUCATE HIM

A tugboat captain acquaintance once asked me a personal question. "Katie, tell me why you are hiding. You're a beautiful girl. Why are you hiding behind all that fat?"

I was nineteen, and I still hated myself . . . well, not myself but my *fat* self. I probably answered him with a weak "I don't know." But I do know that his comment got me wondering if I *was* hiding . . . that maybe I was afraid to be a *thin* beautiful woman. HA! That theory lasted about as long as my next diet!

Now I wish I could go back in time and take the opportunity to educate that tugboat captain. He had seemed sincere enough in his question, as though maybe he had really cared and would have been open to hearing the true answer, which is: "I'm not hiding. If I was hiding, I'd be at home in front of the TV. Instead, I'm out living life, making the best of the hand I was dealt. This is who I am. If you really want to know why I'm fat, sit down and I'll tell you."

We all have our own reasons for being big, and sometimes it's right to explain why, to help educate those who don't understand and who genuinely care, to correct and put an end to the old, wrong stereotypes about big people. More than likely, you've heard a lot of these fallacies, such as "Man, you must eat all the time!" or "It's not healthy to be big." To set these people straight, you have to educate yourself first. Start by reading some of the books I've listed under Exploding Fat Fallacies in the "Resources" section. Memorize facts such as:

- You can be fat *and* fit.
- Research has shown that it's healthier to be 20 percent overweight than 10 percent underweight.
- There are lots of reasons people are overweight, and

overeating is only one of them. Some people are fat because of heredity. Some have a medical condition. Some gain weight because they have to use a certain medication. For others, it's a metabolism problem. If you've never had a weight problem and can easily drop five or ten pounds whenever you want, it's difficult to understand what it's like for someone who practically starves herself and still can't lose weight. Finally, some heavy people *choose* to be heavy because they just feel better that way. As Wynonna Judd once put it, "When I was thin, I was cranky. It ain't worth it."

TELL HIM TO SHUT UP IN A NICE WAY

Two highly regarded therapists in the body-acceptance field, Sally Stosahl, M.A., and Cheri K. Erdman, Ed.D., recommend this polite and simple but no-nonsense response to negative comments about your weight: "My body, my business." Both also recommend that you prepare yourself for negative comments . . . whether you're headed for a visit home, to a class reunion, or even to the local mall. Wrote Sally in *BBW*, "Thinking ahead, equipping ourselves with options and strategies is smart and increases our ability to feel good about ourselves. Let the anticipatory anxiety and fear or dread move you to protect yourself so you can feel empowerment."

One way to do this, according to Cheri, is to actually practice responses like "My body, my business" with a friend until you become comfortable standing up for yourself. Cheri, author of *Live Large!* and *Nothing to Lose*, says that sticking up for yourself in this way becomes even easier if you silently repeat this affirmation to yourself—especially if you feel threatened: "I deserve to be treated with dignity and respect."

KILLER COMEBACKS

If someone is particularly nasty to you and you simply want to cut the offender down to size, so to speak, memorize the all-purpose insult I used as the name of this chapter: "Yeah, well you're ugly and stupid and you can't diet that away!" And here are some other zingers, courtesy of my friend—and former *BBW* editor—Janey Milstead. I've adapted these from an article she wrote for *BBW*.

THE SITUATION: You get heckled in a supermarket checkout line.

THE STRATEGY: Look for something unusual about the person and use it against him! For example, this very situation happened to Janey in L.A. Her tormentor was wearing, of all things, lederhosen (German leather shorts with suspenders).

THE COMEBACK: "You must be the Alpine ignoramus that got loose from the zoo." (She reports that the store fell apart laughing.)

ALTERNATE COMEBACK (should he have, perhaps, a big nose but no lederhosen): "If I had a nose like that I'd keep it out of other people's business, and I'd also have a couple of pounds of it removed."

THE SITUATION: A carload of teenage boys drives by and hoots about your body.

THE STRATEGY: Use what police officers refer to as the "digital spasm": Flip those suckers off! The twist is . . . while you're holding that middle finger high, give 'em a big, friendly smile. "It totally confuses them," Janey reports gleefully.

THE SITUATION: As you take your seat in a movie theater, the person behind you loudly remarks to his date that "All that fat is disgusting."

THE COMEBACK: "It's not my fat that you hate, it's yourself. And you have every reason to."

THE SITUATION: Some weenie sidles up to you at a bar and says, "Oh, baby, we're gonna do so-and-so all night long after you lose that weight!"
THE COMEBACK: "I wouldn't do so-and-so with you if I weighed a hundred pounds and the entire human species was in dire danger of extinction."

THE SITUATION: You're in a particularly hissy mood when someone says that tired old line that always ends with a sigh: "But you have such a pretty face . . ."
THE COMEBACK: "Well, you don't."

THE SITUATION: Someone you really can't insult—your Uncle Roy, for example—remarks, "Hey, you've really gotten fat!"
THE STRATEGY/COMEBACK: Dive into your purse and pull out a mirror. Then gaze at yourself in astonishment and say, "My God, when did this happen?"

THE SITUATION: Another little scene in which you can't afford to be too mean—Aunt Agnes says, "Now, honey, I'm not going to cut you a piece of pie and you know why!"
THE COMEBACK: "Yes, Aunt Agnes, I am going to have a piece of pumpkin pie just like everybody else. And if you say one more word about what I'm eating, I'm going to take off all my clothes and sit on your front porch."

THE SITUATION: In front of a crowd, someone starts making cutting remarks about your body.
THE STRATEGY: Now, this one takes guts, but Janey says it's a real show stopper—and that's what you want to do . . .

stop his show. Burst into great, gulping, heaving, boo-hoo-hoo sobs and torrents of tears. Can't fake the tears? Perform behind a large hankie. The crowd will turn on the perpetrator within seconds.

THE SITUATION: You're back up at the buffet table and some fool says, "Man, you eat all the time!"
THE STRATEGY/COMEBACK: Look as powerful, mean, and hungry as you can. Then say, "I'm a vegetarian, but in your case, I'll make an exception."

THE SITUATION: Someone behind you comments on your derriere.
THE COMEBACK: "Okay, let's take a vote and see which is the biggest—my butt or your mouth!"

WHEN HE SAYS "SORRY, NOT INTERESTED"
You have to handle rejection from guys who turn you down in a different way. Let's say you walk up to a stranger and say my number-one favorite opening line: "Hi!" If he doesn't say hi back, or if he says it and then turns away, say, "Bye! Have a good time!" in a friendly voice. Then casually walk away. You save face, and your real thoughts—about what a hot-looking babe he is and that you'd like to spend the rest of your life with him—will remain your secret forever.

What if he responds to your greeting with something mean? This has happened in the past to my friend Eleni, whose favorite opening line is "I think you're very attractive and I'd like to sit next to you and have a conversation over a drink if you don't mind." Once, a guy gave her a look that simply said, "Are you crazy? You have the nerve to come up to me, Mr. Hot Shit, and ask me if you can sit down next to me? Who do you think you are?" On another occasion, in Eleni's native New Orleans, "where men tend to be crass," she says, a man responded to her suggestion with "Get away from me, fat bitch." Here's how Eleni masterfully handled these incidents: She just walked away without a word. If you respond with an insult in such situations, he's likely to zing you back. And you want to avoid more ego damage. Just move on to your next prospect.

Things get a little more complicated if the object of your affection is someone you already know. After all, if he turns you down, you're going to be running into him—or even working at the next desk—for months or years to come. Before you cast your net, make sure you feel some kind of vibe coming back from him whenever you happen to meet him. I've said it before in this book: Women have superior skills in translating nonverbal communication. Just keep in mind that this radar system isn't infallible.

Consider this situation: You ask the guy out on a casual date and he says he can't make it that night, but he does not unequivocally indicate "Not interested. Period." Don't push him to reschedule; be cool. Just say, "Maybe another time" and change the subject. Then wait as long as you can possibly stand it before asking him out again (and we're talking about a couple of *weeks* here—not minutes or days!). In the meantime, maybe he'll ask *you* out. If he doesn't, and he responds to your next date pitch in the same noncommittal way, just stay cool and continue to give him reminders now and then (by staring a bit too long, letting your hand graze his, etc.). There's a strong possibility that something could come of this if you're just patient.

Now, what if he says something like, "No, thanks. Sorry, but I'm just not interested in that kind of relationship with you"? Don't get angry at him. Don't cause a scene. Don't stop talking to him. Simply say, "No harm done" in a friendly tone and continue to be friendly. If you find yourself thinking about him, change the channel in your brain and get out there and set your sights on someone else!

SOME COMFORTING WORDS ABOUT REJECTION

Finally, here are some words of wisdom from famous minds—proving that *everyone* faces rejection now and then. You are not alone, and you, too, can move on.

> *Your life is not on the line. Your worth, success, or self-esteem do not depend on the response of the other person. If your approach is positive, friendly, considerate, and respectful, the response you get will generally be the same. The answer to your proposal of future contact may be a negative one, but the way in which it is delivered should generally be kind. If it is not, that means that the other person has a problem; you don't.*
>
> —Stephen M. Johnson,
> *First Person Singular*

> *Being rejected does not make you worthless. There are many reasons why any given person might not be interested in either your initiation or in future contact with you. Many of these reasons have little or nothing to do with you, and you should manage as well as possible not to take them seriously. To gain anything worthwhile, you must take some risks. Being rejected is a risk that you will be taking in this endeavor, but rejection is not the end of the world. In dealing with it, you may learn some important things about yourself and about life.*
>
> —Stephen M. Johnson,
> *First Person Singular*

> *Finish every day and be done with it. You have done what you could. Some blunders and absurdities no doubt crept in; forget them as soon as you can. Tomorrow is a new day; begin it well and serenely and with too high a spirit to be cumbered*

with your old nonsense. This day is all that is good and fair. It is too dear, with its hopes and invitations, to waste a moment on the yesterdays.

> —Ralph Waldo Emerson,
> "One Day at a Time"

The world goes up and the world goes down,
  And the sunshine follows the rain;
And yesterday's sneer and yesterday's frown
  Can never come over again.

> —Charles Kingsley,
> "Songs"

My answer to the question would be this: "It's finally not important what other people think."

> —Cher, when asked by an audience of
> UCLA students "What are some of your
> insights about life?"

Pay no attention to derogatory remarks about you. The person who carried the message may not be the world's most accurate reporter. . . . Insecurity (or a stomachache, a toothache, or a headache) is often at the root of most backbiting.

> —Ann Landers

It sometimes helps to remember that everyone who had the chance criticized Madame Curie, Socrates was given hemlock to drink, and Modigliani was told he didn't know how to paint. All these innovative thinkers were ridiculed and ostracized, and in the final analysis all were terrific contributors to mankind.

> —Cathy Cash Spellman,
> Notes to My Daughters

Even the most relaxed, noncompetitive woman often becomes extremely competitive when it comes to getting men. And I'm sure many of you have experienced this: An insecure *slender* woman goes after a guy who is clearly hooked on a BBW. Why does the thin woman—who might stop and think before encroaching on another thin woman's territory—consider the big woman's guy fair game? Why does she feel an almost compulsive need to go after him—even if, had he been alone, she wouldn't be particularly attracted to him?

Charles Roy Schroeder dissects the roots of this phenomenon very well in his book *Fat Is Not a Four-Letter Word*. He says that staying slim is "a chronically agonizing experience. . . . These miserable feelings may explain why thin women often have such hostile emotions toward fat women—particularly when the latter are happy with themselves and their lives."

He continues: "A woman who elects to chronically suffer from food deprivation and who regularly exercises to exhaustion to conform to the public standards of thinness is understandably not eager to hear that fat women are in reality just as beautiful. . . . It must be a bitter pill for the thin woman whose suffering has not made her happier after all."

I would take this a step further. When a thin woman living in today's society sees a big woman with a great guy, she no doubt wonders, "If he's choosing *her* over me, what's wrong with me? Am I ugly? Are my breasts too small?" and on and on. She doesn't stop to think that he might simply (horrors!) prefer big women or that a woman's size doesn't matter to him at all. No, she assumes he's a fat phobic just like she is, and so she feels compelled to win him over to restore her faith in her own desirability.

Accept this phenomenon as a given. But it's *not* a given that you're going to lose him to Miss Skinny Minnie. Some battlefield tips:

• **Love yourself.** Reread the chapter "How to Feel as Special as You Are" to learn how to do that. Also reread "Why Men Love Big, Beautiful Women" to convince yourself that one thing men love about us is our confidence in, and comfort with, ourselves. As actress/singer/comedian/friend Eleni says, "I've gotten the stares, I've gotten the attitude from friends, acquaintances, and coworkers when I introduce them to my great-looking boyfriend. I can read their minds because it's written all over their faces: 'How can *she* get a boyfriend like that? Why don't I have a boyfriend when I'm thinner than she is?' I think these women feel more threatened than I do, more intimidated than I am because I'm completely comfortable in my own skin."

Eleni continues: "I wish that skinny women knew that they have nothing to be afraid of, and that they could get comfortable in their skin, too. A lot of people don't understand that I can be healthy, happy, in a relationship with a man . . . and still be overweight. They can't understand how I 'landed him' when *I'm* thinking, 'He's lucky to have me!' Ultimately, it's a matter of mentality, how you were raised, what you believe in. If you believe that your body and your looks are all that you have going for you, you're going to have low self-esteem and little self-confidence. I grew up believing that I'm a wonderful person with a good heart, and that I deserve the best in life. I deserve the world as my oyster. And my weight has nothing to do with that."

• **Don't assume he'll like her better.** He may have a preference for bigger women, or size just doesn't matter to him. A big-woman lover I called J.D. in Chapter One won my admiration when he told me that he didn't know if people ever made fun of him for being with a big woman "because my heart and eyes are always on my woman only." He says he's run into the phenomenon of thinner women trying to woo him away from his heftier honey. Says J.D.: "I tell them, 'I'm sorry, but I want to be with *this* girl. There are lots of guys here looking for thin women. I'm sure you'll have no problem attracting them.'"

• **Decide if he's worth fighting over.** Sometimes it's just not worth the effort. "Rock," as I'll call him, was the epitome of the Rock Star—no one woman could ever satisfy him. He had his stable of regulars and an endless list of one-nighters. I'm not proud of doing it, but I was young and naive and starry-eyed: I was a stable member. I liked him and we had great times together, but I always saw him for what he was . . . so I never fell in love with him. I had a good friend at the time who was also young and hot. She was that paradoxical combination—totally vain but insecure at the same time. She was really fun, though, and always made it her goal to have every guy at a party notice and like her. She was forever "friendly flirting" with other girls' guys, and sometimes that flirting went further. One day, as we were sunning on the beach, she asked me whether Rock was a good kisser or not. I didn't hesitate in giving her the go-ahead to find out. I made sure she knew about his ways, that she knew he and I were involved, and that she knew I liked him. But she wanted him anyway, so I said, "Go for it." She did, and she got him—for one night. She freaked out when he didn't call again. She couldn't believe that he hadn't fallen madly in love with her. She felt she was better than me, and she didn't try to hide her shock that he chose to continue to be with me. It made me see her true colors. Regarding this entire incident, I didn't care about him; I was more disappointed in her. It was all about beating me, not winning him. Our friendship will never be the same.

• **Make your move faster than she does.** On a wild girls-only weekend in Rosarito Beach, Mexico, three of us went on the prowl together. The men at the first bar were unappealing—except for one guy I spotted. I blew it by pointing him out to the others. The petite girl in our group decided to vie for his attention, as well. I was winning the game until she broke out the move: She asked what time it was and leaned over to look at his watch while her elbow subtly—and "accidentally"—caressed his crotch. Now, how could I top that? I make my moves, but I never go *that* low. I lost, but graciously . . . in the spirit of the wild weekend. Well . . . let's just say I *still* had a wild weekend!

• **Talk about him.** Men like to talk about themselves and their interests. Who doesn't? You learned in Chapter One that one of the reasons many men prefer big women is that we are less into ourselves than thin women are. Talking with him about him is easy: You ask about his job, sports, what he likes and why. It's also the best way to get to know him and to find out if he's got the package that *you* are looking for.

• **Don't give up so easily!** Don't go overboard trying to win. Guard against being a "Too Much" (see Chapter Two). But don't go to the opposite extreme—that is, don't withdraw to a corner and lick your wounds while Thin Girl moves in for the kill. Here's another Katie story to illustrate: A few years ago, I really liked the new guitarist in a friend's band. One night we ran into each other at a club and spent the evening talking and having a great time. The next week, the same thing happened, and we left together and went on to another club. We were having a blast until a thin chick came over and sat with us. She had met the guitarist just a few weeks earlier, and she immediately started making moves on him as I sat there. He turned to me and said, "I'm sorry about this. I'll ask her to leave." What I should have said was, "Good idea. Thanks!" But, feeling intimidated, idiot me said, "Oh, no, you don't have to do that. It's cool." Then I got up and left the table to join friends on the other side of the room. The guitarist and the other woman started dating and dated for the next year. Meanwhile, he and I developed only a good friendship. He's been through a few girlfriends since then, but we shall forever remain . . . buddies. Dammit! He gave me clear signals that he wanted *me*, but I was too insecure to recognize them and hold my ground.

Listen, girl: You fight for him!

Okay, you read the chapter on "The Approach," you've tried the bars, the library, the sports games. You are out there and just not hooking up. Or maybe you just moved to a new area and aren't familiar enough with your new environment to go it alone. Or perhaps you just don't have the time, energy, or desire to make that much effort, and yet you still want a man with whom to share precious moments. What do you do? 1-2-3, here goes:

DANCES

All over the country, clubs and organizations are hosting parties and dances specifically for bigger women and men who like them that way. I attended two such events—one in Los Angeles and one in New York—and they couldn't have been more different. One was great, the other not—which means that before you accept any invitation be sure to do as much research as possible: Who is organizing the event? How much does it cost and where does the money go? Is charity involved? Do you know others who have gone to this specific event before?

Here's an example of what happens when you don't do the research. The invitation read "House Party Dance Mixer," and I received it at a plus-size networking luncheon—so I just assumed it would be okay.

I convinced two plus-size friends to join me. We got all decked out—three young, hip, foxy big women (sizes 18 to 22) heading out convinced we would steal the show! We drove an hour in L.A. in pouring rain and walked through a gutter river to a little pink house glowing with Christmas lights. We were greeted by a middle-aged, very casually dressed, very friendly woman. She welcomed us and asked for a $15 per person donation toward party expenses and a charity fund. I had paid a $15 cover to get into the hottest clubs in the country, but never for a house party! I bargained her down to three for the price of two—after all, we had driven an hour to get there. I figured we'd go in, dry off, scope it out, have a drink, and split.

Well, we walked into the living room to find five super-size women sitting around watching the Olympics! We quickly went into the kitchen and found a few other women and the gourmet refreshments—Cheetos, carrot cake, and warm apple cider. I asked if there was a bar, and the hostess broke out a gallon jug of Chablis, complete with a twist-off cap. I opted for the cider and chatted with the women in the kitchen. They told us that the organization sponsoring the party wasn't a membership club, but it did have many regulars. And they all agreed that this particular night's party was a major flop. They advised my friends and me that the hotel parties sponsored by the same group are much more fun, because they attract more people—especially more *men*, who were nowhere to be found! I asked where the dancing at *this* party was supposed to be (after all, it had said "dance" on the invitation). They pointed toward the garage, but I had to go through the pouring rain to get there. I just had to see if there was anyone else at this happenin' party. Nope. And no decorations, no music, no nothing—it was just a garage. Back to the kitchen.

Two men finally arrived. One, a supersize guy, immediately joined the couch-bound women in the living room. The other made a beeline for the kitchen. All of our new friends seemed to know, and loathe, this guy. He made lame attempts at flirting with each of us in turn. He was too busy staring at your chest or at the rear end of the girl walking past. He was a "chubby chaser," the type of guy all big women hold in contempt—the kind of guy who ruins it for the normal guys who really do like big women. His lines didn't change from one girl to the next. What a major loser!

The lesson to be learned from that nightmare of a night is to be aware and to ask questions before you go. Had I only called the club's information line, I might have learned that this was to be quite literally a house party and that "mixer" meant an event where you can talk easily. In other words, no music.

But don't let my experience turn you off to the idea. For years I've been hearing about a great dance club in Los Angeles called the Big Difference. This group hosts "Big" events about once a month . . . and some feature live entertainment and/or a fashion show. The women I know who have attended say that the events are a lot of fun and attract about 300 people.

New York City has the reputation of being home to the best clubs in America. That goes for the big-women club scene, as well. While in New York to meet our editor, my cowriter and I joined club locals Donald and Kelly (the rap singers you met in Chapter One) to check out a dance hosted by Large Encounters. This was held in a nice bar with a definite "club scene" feel to it. I don't know if it was because we were with a couple of popular locals, but everyone was extremely friendly. My cowriter insists that a few of the women were shooting daggerlike looks my way—

and she's probably right about that, since I had heard that some women who attend these events become very domineering about their territory and don't like to see new women, especially smaller plus-size women. One myth—a myth I believed until I finally attended these functions—is that they attract only supersize women. Not true. At the L.A. party and especially the one in New York, I saw women of all sizes. Even my skinny cowriter didn't stick out. Another observation I made at the New York event: All the women in attendance looked great! Each was decked out in her own personal style and each pulled it off nicely.

There were, however, two things that bothered me about the New York dance: The lights were too bright and there were too many chairs. I'm used to dark clubs, where lighting sets the mood and emphasizes the music. And if there are chairs, people will sit, and how do you meet anyone if you're sitting down? How can anyone see you if you're sitting? It's a lot harder to get on the dance floor from a chair.

But here's a real plus for the Large Encounters event: The men outnumbered the women! And there were men of all kinds—including several real lookers. Tall, short, young, old, aggressive, shy—it was a very diverse crowd. I got asked to dance a few times, but I also watched eagerly from the sidelines, waiting to be asked. At a regular club, I would have just gone out and danced alone, but here the lights were so bright that I felt intimidated. A passing wave of insecurity—it happens to us all!

Lora White describes her first big-woman dance—at Southeast Super Singles in Atlanta—as her own personal coming-out party. She had to overcome a lot of doubts and fears before attending, but finally racked up the courage and went it alone. She said everyone was friendly and she had a great time just enjoying people. "By the end of the night," she reports, "I was approached by five men! From then on, I knew I looked good and I've never had a problem getting men since." It took that particular environment to show her that she had what it took all along. All she needed was a little confidence. After that night, she had the courage to go out, to *regular* clubs, and on each occasion someone offered to buy her a drink. (Lora, by the way, has become so fervent about size acceptance that she's started an organization called Big Options—see "Resources" for the address—that provides classes and printed information for people of size on how they can learn to feel "I'm a good person" and "I can have a fulfilling life at any size.")

Where can you find out about big women dances and clubs? If you subscribe to a magazine for large women, or you're on the mailing list of a plus-size clothing store, you'll probably receive invitations and notices of events when sponsors buy the mailing lists of these businesses. Many such sponsors also advertise in magazines for large women. If you're hooked up to the Internet, you can use one of the popular search engines, typing in something like "big women events" as the search phrase. You'll find lots of Web pages of events. The main search engines and their addresses are:

- Webcrawler (http://webcrawler.com)
- Lycos (http://www.lycos.com)
- Alta Vista (http://altavista.digital.com)
- Yahoo! (http://yahoo.com)

THE PERSONALS

Recently I was in a rut, going through a major man dry spell. My cowriter urged me to run a personal ad. I was really uncomfortable with the idea, but she convinced me that this has become the norm in the nineties—it's not just sleazy, desperate types who are advertising. She even wrote the ad for me: "SUCCESSFUL PLUS-SIZE MODEL, big, beautiful, blue-eyed blond with great sense of humor. Seeks tall, handsome, fun, outgoing WM, 28–40." It ran for four weeks in *L.A. Weekly* (an entertainment-oriented, alternative newspaper), and I got five calls, which is not a lot, but the point is that it takes only one. Three of the guys sounded too weird in their voice-mail responses, but I did connect with the other two, and even though they lacked something, the experiences were good to have nonetheless.

The first date, Steve, had just moved to Los Angeles and worked in the entertainment industry. He told me that this was his first experience with personal ads, and he had chosen my ad because he liked bigger women. We talked for over an hour; he seemed nice and normal, so we agreed to meet for a drink. As soon as I saw him, I realized I should have paid a little more attention to the way he described himself. I'm five foot ten (six feet in heels), and let's just say over 200 pounds. Compared to me, a guy who is six feet tall and weighs 150 pounds is tiny! Nonetheless he was cute and sweet, and we did have a nice time, but it was definitely not a love connection.

The second guy seemed a little deeper than the first. An accomplished jazz musician and an intellectual, Keith had a matter-of-fact attitude that was a refreshing change from Steve's please-like-me persona. Keith was an avid bicyclist and didn't mind when I said I wasn't, so we met for dinner. At the restaurant, I learned that he was *so* avid a bicyclist that he didn't even own a car! That set off warning lights: A guy without a car in L.A. has got to be a bit off! He was nice looking, but I had a hard time getting over the fact that he was wearing Birkenstocks with long pants (a personal dislike of mine). Over dinner Keith said that my ad had caught his attention because I seemed so open about the kind of guy I was looking for. "You sounded like you'd enjoy meeting someone just for the experience," Keith said. Well, that's true to a degree.

After dinner, we went for a walk. We stopped to take in the view of the lights of Los Angeles, and I noticed that he kept standing on his toes. I suspected he had lied to me when he'd told me he was six feet tall. Eventually, he made the move: He took a step toward me so that his body touched mine. I coolly took two steps backward. He tried again. This time, as I stepped back, I said, "I'm sorry, I'm just not feeling that vibe." As we said goodnight he said he'd call, and we both knew he wouldn't.

Just because my two encounters were not love connections, it doesn't mean yours won't be. Consider these examples for a moment. Two large-size friends, Rhonda and Denise, have had a lot of success with personal ads—both in placing their own and in responding to others. Rhonda went out with someone she met through the ads for more than a year. They were even talking marriage, but their inability to agree on the issue of children (she wanted them, he didn't) recently broke up the relationship. Denise is still dating two of the more than fifty guys who answered an ad she placed seven months ago. "I'm just not ready to choose between them," she says with a blissful smile.

Denise, Rhonda, and I spent most of a Saturday coming up with tips—based on our experiences—to help you find a prince among the toads through the personals:

WHERE TO ADVERTISE AND/OR TO READ ADS

Certainly you can advertise as well as respond to the personal ads in magazines for large women or their admirers. *Dimensions* magazine, for example, is packed with personals. There are also on-line personals especially for big women and their admirers. One is #BBW (not affiliated with the magazine). Visit the group's Web site (http://www.momi.com.default.htlm) to place a free personal ad or just to browse. Another on-line personals service aimed at big women and men (in this case, they mean "well hung"!) "of size" is called Big Date. Buxom and "big, beautiful women" are invited to run their ads for free. See Big Date's Web site for more info (http://www.big-date.com).

However, don't bypass more traditional personal-ad outlets, such as your daily newspaper. To be sure, you'll find crass types who state, in no uncertain terms, that "fatties" need not apply. And more civilized sorts will specify the same thing with polite euphemisms such as "slender," "slim," "petite," "fit" (being unaware that you can be fat *and* fit), and "weight proportionate to height." But sit down one afternoon and read *all* of a major newspaper's ads under "Men Seeking Women." You'll find at least a half-dozen advertisers who are specifically seeking a larger woman, and at least another half-dozen more who obviously don't care about body type because they don't even mention it. ("Be careful, though, of guys who say stuff like 'age, looks, weight, race unimportant,'" advises Denise. "Generally, I've found that these guys are simply desperate for sex.")

Denise places and responds to ads only in the *Los Angeles Times*. "I'm pretty highly educated—an MBA—and I figure that the educated men I like to hook up with are more likely to advertise in—and to *read*—a daily newspaper. The guys who advertise or answer ads in the alternative weeklies or in shoppers like *The Pennysaver* are not for me."

Rhonda has a more democratic approach. She has advertised and responded to ads in a variety of media and is particularly fond of on-line personals, "mainly because you're not limited to, say, three lines, like you are in a newspaper," she says. "You can be as prolific as you want! Another advantage: You don't have to talk to the guy right off. You can get to know him better through several e-mail exchanges."

There are other big advantages to searching the Net for sweeties. First, you'll find more than 200 sites offering on-line personals. And, as *Fortune* magazine put it, ". . . most Web surfers are college-educated men with healthy incomes." Furthermore, Jennifer Johnson of Web-Personals says there's an even higher ratio of male-to-female users on her personals site than the three to one population using the Internet as a whole. "The traffic on WebPersonals is 80 percent men and 20 percent women," she said recently.

WebPersonals (http://www.webpersonals.com) is one of Rhonda's favorite browsing fields. She also likes http://Match.com; http://LoveSearch.com; and http://swoon.com, the latter brought to you by the people who publish *Glamour*, *Mademoiselle*, *GQ*, and *Details* magazines.

HOW TO WRITE AN AD

Whether you're writing an ad for print, composing a voice-mail ad, or going on-line with your pitch, Denise, Rhonda, I, and others offer this advice:

• Itemize what Gail Prince, who runs a singles support group in Chicago, calls the "nonnegotiables." "[That's] what you absolutely must have in a person, and what you'll never accept," she told *Cosmopolitan* magazine.

• "Dateable people run ads that stress physical attractiveness and superficialities," psychologist Basha Blumenthal-Kaplan, who runs singles groups, told *Cosmo*. "Mateable people are more likely to run ads in which they talk about their values, interests, and desire for friendship."

• Use *exact* words. Terms like "beautiful" (yes, I know I used that in my ad) are too broad. Be more specific, such as "golden-haired, golden eyes, golden-hearted." At the same time, be just as precise when stating your requirements for a man. As I learned, everybody has a different definition of "tall." Some guys think they're tall at five ten. Replace "tall" with "6-foot-2 and over."

• Include an age range with a *definite* cutoff. If you say "over 35," you'll hear from lots of guys who could have gone to high school with your dad—the sixty-somethings.

• Don't sound desperate. As *Cosmo* put it, "Women who advertise for a 'long-term commitment' sound needy. Men often use that line because they think it's what women want to hear."

• Be creative and memorable. Please don't waste words on stuff like "I like puppies, sunsets, walking on the beach." Really, who *doesn't*? Better to include a line from a favorite song or poem to make your ad stand out. Rhonda once ran an ad that was headlined "Must know what 'Inna-Gada-Da-Vida' is!" Almost every voice-mail respondent started his pitch by singing a few bars from that late-1960s Iron Butterfly song. It gave Rhonda a perfect opening for her telephoned response, i.e., "You sing terribly, but I'll forgive that, since you sound so interesting anyway . . ."

WHAT DO YOU SAY ABOUT YOUR BODY SIZE?

There are two schools of thought here. Gloria Brame, author of the *Cosmopolitan* book called *Where the Boys Are*, wrote that "If you're seriously worried that you are too fat to get the man you want, just leave the information out. . . . If you simply omit the detail that makes you uneasy, the man answering the ad will know he's taking a chance that you don't fit some imaginary ideal, and he will be more likely to accept you as you truly are." Further, she advises that you "focus on your hobbies, interests, or personal qualities, and *not* on the way you look. . . . Men are *more* likely to respond to ads that have a bit of mystery."

Rhonda, Denise, and I beg to differ. Men are visual creatures. Sorry, but they are much less forgiving about a first visual impression. In our experience, in a first phone conversation, if a guy doesn't already know about your body size, he will ask something like, "Are you small, medium, or big?" or even, "How much do you weigh?" If you don't tell him, if you answer him with something like, "I have no idea how much I weigh," you may be setting yourself up for some real hurt and humiliation upon that first person-to-person meeting. Rhonda demurred about her size with the first personal ad she ever answered, and the subsequent meeting was a disaster. "I walked into the bar where we had arranged to meet," she says. "I saw the guy—he was exactly as he'd described himself. But when he saw me, he looked away. When I approached him and said, 'Are you Jonathan?' he replied, 'No, my name is Richard' and turned back to his drink. As the old saying goes, I didn't need to walk out the door of that bar—I felt so diminished, I simply walked under it."

Heavy guys have always used a wonderful euphemism to describe themselves in their personal ads. They call themselves "teddy bear types." Doesn't that sound lovable and cuddly? Well, we can use euphemisms, too, and, believe me, guys know the shorthand. Try "Rubenesque"—for the painter who adored bigger women—or "voluptuous" or "full-figured." A phrase that has always worked for Denise is "plenty of soft curves." Don't use: chubby, plump, big-boned, or—the worst—don't say how much you weigh. Also, don't use terms that many people won't define correctly. Marcia Millman, author of *Such a Pretty Face* (see "Resources") once used the word "zaftig" to describe herself in an ad in New York's *Village Voice*. "About 20 percent of the callers didn't know what zaftig meant." (It's a Yiddish word meaning "having a full, shapely figure.") A friend of Rhonda's tried the word "Amazon"—most of the responses she got were from guys who described themselves as "submissive." They thought Amazon meant "dominatrix."

MORE TIPS FOR WRITING AN AD

• Keep it short. If you write a huge ad, you'll look desperate, and if you list too many of your own wonderful qualities, you'll sound as though you have an ego problem. Listing too many of the qualities you insist on in a man may scare some decent guys off. The essentials: your age, race, sex, and marital status. Use abbreviations. Here are the ones most personal-ad perusers are familiar with:

DWF: Divorced white female
SWF: Single white female
DWM: Divorced white male
SWM: Single white male
DBF: Divorced black female
DBM: Divorced black male

D: Divorced

WW: Widowed woman

J: Jewish

C: Christian/Catholic

A: Asian

NA: Native American

H: Hispanic

Bi: Bisexual

D/DF: Drug and disease free

NS: Nonsmoker

NS/ND: Nonsmoker/Nondrinker

NS/LD: Nonsmoker/Light drinker

P: Professional

LTR: Long-term relationship

ISO: In search of

FA: Fat admirer (used in the personals in magazines for or in celebration of big women)

• If the personals service you're using is one in which interested guys respond by mail, rent a post office box. It's really a cheap investment for safety's sake.

• If you need to leave your phone number with interesting respondents, give your work phone number. If you work at home or are unemployed, change your answering machine message so that it doesn't reveal your name.

• Does your personal ad require you to record a voice-mail message? Write out a script beforehand and practice saying it a few times so you sound natural when you record it. Make sure it fits into the service's specified time limit—usually thirty seconds to two minutes—by timing it. Last, but not least, ask respondents to repeat their phone numbers *twice*. You'll be amazed at how many guys—in their nervousness—forget to leave their phone number or say it in such a rush that you can't make out some of the numbers.

• Screen your respondents carefully. Some things should set off alarm bells: a guy who is unemployed, one who talks too much about his ex-wife or mother, or someone who gets too sexual right off the bat, i.e., "What's your favorite position?"

• When you talk to him by phone, ask the questions that are important to you. You own and love five cats? Ask if he's allergic to them. You're fanatically prochoice? Ask where he stands on that issue.

• If he sounds like a total loser or just doesn't seem compatible, let him down nicely. Just be honest: "I don't think we're compatible." Then massage his ego: "But I'm sure the right woman is out there for a guy as interesting as you are."

RESPONDING TO *HIS* AD

• Rhonda feels men essentially tell the truth about themselves in ads but leave out the less stellar stuff. For example, she once responded to an ad in which the guy described himself as "a blond, blue-eyed, lifeguard type." "And he *was*," Rhonda says, "except that he'd been unemployed for five years!" Avoid this type of surprise by casually asking what he does for a living, as well as about his hobbies and interests.

• Don't be dull. Parroting back his own likes, such as "I'm really into Rollerblading, horses, and Anne Rice novels, too" is about as creative a response as an advertiser saying he likes—yawn!—"puppies, sunsets, and walks on the beach." Just say you seem to have a lot in common and mention some of your own interests, too.

• Also tell him your first name, what in his ad compelled

you to respond, what you do for a living, and give him your phone number.

MEETING HIM FOR THE FIRST TIME

• *Always* meet him somewhere that's safe, familiar to you, and public. And preferably in the daytime.

• Let a friend know where you're going and when you expect to be back.

• Get there on your own—via public transportation or your own car. This gives you the option of leaving whenever *you* want to.

• Let the guy know in advance that you have only an hour to spend with him, and that you've already made plans to meet a girl pal for a movie later on. This will give you an airtight excuse to leave if the guy turns out to be a jerk or loser. And if he's the man of your dreams? You'll leave him longing for more of your time.

• Also tell him in advance that you'll be wearing or carrying something that's easy to spot—such as a pink scarf or a red jacket. Denise always tells guys she'll be carrying a *Cosmopolitan* magazine. In this way, you'll spare the guy the agony of asking every tall blonde, "Are you Katie?"

• Break the ice by asking thought-provoking questions that require more than a yes or no answer. For example: "What is your favorite TV show?" or "What do you think is the best rock song of all time?" or "What do you like about the work you do?" Avoid asking him about his finances, however ("What are you currently making?"). At best you'll sound like an interviewer from his human resources department. At worst, he'll see dollar signs in your eyes!

• Be nice even if you don't like him or there's no chemistry on your part. Just end the evening with something vague like "Maybe we can get together sometime in the future." Any man with an ounce of intelligence will recognize this as a nice, polite kiss-off. "I wish guys would adopt this civilized mode of farewell, too," says Denise. "I once had a guy mutter, 'You said you were buxom—but you're really not. You're just *proportionate!*' before he stomped angrily out of the restaurant. He said 'You're just proportionate' in the same tone one might say 'You just have the plague.' It would have been so much easier on my ego if he'd simply used that civilized but standard male kiss-off: 'I'll call you.'"

• Don't drink too much. Even Quasimodo starts to look good after a few Long Island iced teas.

MATCHMAKING SERVICES

They may not seem as contemporary as on-line personals, but matchmaking services are still around and worth a try. Today's services are more high-tech versions of the computer-profile matching services of the sixties and seventies. With some, like Single Search(http://nsns.com/single-search/), you fill out a profile on the computer, conduct searches on-line, and respond to matches by e-mail. Other services that have great word of mouth include Lisa the Matchmaker (http://matchme.com/quest.html) and the famous Great Expectations, with offices practically everywhere, which enables you—and your prospective beaus—to see pictures and videos of each other before you even agree to meet. NAAFA (the National Association to Advance Fat Acceptance) runs a computer dating service specifically for big women and their admirers. For more information, write to NAAFA at Box 188620, Sacramento, CA, 95818, or call (916) 558-6880.

All of the above services are reputable and well established, but be aware that not *all* such services are. There are no federal guidelines regulating this industry. Sometimes a service will collect a hefty fee and simply match you with someone who has nothing more in common with you than your religion. Other companies lie about their membership numbers or have no refund or cancellation policies. The Better Business Bureau of New York offers these tips:

- Ask: How long have you been in business?
- How are candidates screened?
- Do you have a refund and/or cancellation policy?
- Scrutinize the profile questionnaire carefully. Will it accurately represent you?
- Call your local Better Business Bureau to determine if any complaints have been lodged against the service.
- Read your contract carefully. If there's a lawyer in the family, consult him/her!

WHERE TO FIND MATCHMAKING SERVICES

- They often advertise in local free, university, and alternative newspapers. You can also find them in the classified ad sections of city magazines like *New York* and *Philadelphia.*
- In the Yellow Pages. You'll find the most established services here.
- On the Internet. Use the search engines listed earlier in this chapter. Type in search terms like "singles," "matchmakers," and "dating services."

SEARCHING THE INTERNET

There's another place I recommend going to meet men: Chat rooms on the various services like AOL and CompuServe. I haven't had the chance to visit any of these myself, but Kat, one of my best friends, swears by them. For months she has been raving about Dan, an amazing guy she met on-line and with whom she is falling in love. He lives in Wyoming and she lives in California, but they meet each other every night for intimate written conversations in an AOL chat room.

I'll never forget her excitement when they spoke by phone for the first time. He had asked her to "log off" (that is, to open her phone line), and then he called. She says she has never been so excited to hear someone's voice. It was the weeks of anticipation that had got her going. One time, he surprised her by ordering Chinese food to be delivered to her house. They shared that Chinese dinner together—thousands of miles apart. What a true romantic Dan is!

They had exchanged photographs of themselves over the Net, and both were extremely pleased. But Kat had a secret: The photo she sent Dan was taken at a time when she was the thinnest she'd ever been. Finally, she broke down and told him that she was bigger than she was in the picture. He said it didn't matter. With that, and as their relationship continued to grow, she got the courage to send him a more recent and realistic photo. I was with her as she panicked, nervously waiting for him to get back to her about the photo. She had all kinds of crazy, negative thoughts about what his reaction might be. Finally, he wrote back to her and said he liked the new photo better than the old one and that he was even more attracted to her!

Interestingly, Kat didn't meet Dan in a "big woman" chat room. In fact, she had never visited any of the big-women chat rooms until I asked her to check them out for me. (Her basic opinion: Most of the talk is sex-oriented.)

She found Dan by finding chat rooms organized around her own interests like *The X-Files* and reincarnation. Think of your own interests, and then follow Kat's example. You'll find a guy who already has a great deal in common with you!

When you're part of a big family in a small town, you know practically everybody and everybody knows you. It's hard to find guys appealing when you've known them since they were wetting their pants in preschool. And no doubt the feeling is mutual!

But I learned how to solve this problem when I was a teen. I loved to just drive around San Clemente with my friends. On one particular night of cruisin', we met some surfers from out of town who were camping for the weekend. Keep in mind that when I was in high school, surfers were considered high-status dates. They were gorgeous and friendly, and they liked us! One of them asked for my phone number, and we started seeing each other. He lived about an hour away and would come down to San Clemente to surf and see me. He often brought friends, who hit it off with my friends. All of this helped me get through what otherwise probably would have been awkward and lonely high school dating years. I didn't have to worry about convincing the guy next door that I had grown up, that I was no longer the fat girl who used to beat him up! That's why I feel it's important to get out and meet new people.

A few years later, I discovered that in order to meet men, it's also helpful to change environments—to get out and see the world. On a diving trip to the Great Barrier Reef I became friends with an Englishman named Jerry. He was traveling the globe and very candidly admitted that his mission was to "experience the women of the world." I varied the wording of Jerry's mission and made it my own: I was going to meet the men of the world! (Interesting footnote: When I visited Jerry in his hometown of Eastbourne after he'd finished his world travels, he was dating a local girl!)

I'll never forget my first solo excursion. I had just turned eighteen and was planning a trip to Hawaii with a friend. At the last minute, my friend canceled on me, and I had to decide whether to go alone or stay home. Not only did I go, but, as I recounted in the Introduction, I ended up living there with five surfers on Kauai for four months. Before I left the Mainland, I quit my job as a salesclerk at Lane Bryant, told my parents I might be gone for two weeks or two months or two years, and took off!

It was on that very trip, at Los Angeles International Airport, that I received my first-ever compliment from a stranger. A skycap told me I was beautiful. Now, I'd been told I had a "beautiful face" before but never simply . . . "beautiful." That's when it first hit me that when you leave your familiar environment, and leave your history behind, you can really reinvent yourself. And, in many parts of the world, your size is considered an asset by men—*not* a defect. Here's where to find blokes who love bountiful babes:

DOWN UNDER

Australia has intrigued me ever since I was a child. In high school, I swore I'd visit the country by the time I was twenty-one. Then an Australian boy who was a classmate of mine in San Clemente told me that Australian women are treated like second-class citizens by Australian men. That news made me hesitate about going, but in the end I just couldn't resist. Australian men are big, funny, smart, and macho—and that's the kind I like! I found Australia to be very romantic, and I was delighted that the culture down there is like California's—outdoorsy, athletic. But the best news for us big women is that you don't have to be a skinny beach babe to attract men as is the case in southern California. And the Aussie guys treated me like gold . . . not like a second-class citizen. Maybe that was because I'm American, or because they were impressed that I had the guts to travel alone. Either way, I love Australia.

To further illustrate this point: Australia is the only country I've ever visited in which stores carry sizes 1 to 52—and large sizes aren't relegated to the basement, either.

I met a great guy in **New Zealand**, too, but New Zealand was more memorable for what it taught me about different cultures—how our way of life isn't the only way and maybe not even the best. For example, the guy I met took me on an exhilarating Jeep ride down one of the runways at the airport in Wellington, New Zealand's capital. Incredibly, there were no fences around those runways, so we just drove right on and then into a airplane hangar, where we sped right under a parked Air New Zealand plane.

I gasped at the freedom of it all. "Anybody could climb up on this plane and plant a bomb!" I said to him. "There's no security!"

"How bloody American!" he replied. "That's the way you people think, and that's why you have the problems you have!" Which reminds me of a quote I keep in my Daytimer (though I can't remember where I got it): "A tourist is someone who goes to affirm his own vision of the world. A traveler is someone who goes to discover another vision of the world that opposes his own." Be a traveler.

HAWAII AND OTHER PACIFIC ISLANDS

Wherever you find large populations of ethnic **Hawaiians** and **Samoans,** you'll find lots of big women, and men who love them. The men also tend to be big—being "of size" is apparently both a genetically determined and culturally supported trait. Before I left San Clemente to live on Kauai, all of my well-traveled surfer buddies told me, "You'll do well there, Katie. Hawaiians like big people." It was true—and so different from southern California. People were filled with the spirit of *aloha,* and they were neither as competitive nor as judgmental as Californians.

THE BAHAMAS

Size doesn't appear to be an issue in **Nassau,** the Bahamas, either. A majority of the local women are big, and I saw plenty of large-sized American women tourists dancing on the beaches with abandon, and without covering up. In **Georgetown** on the island of **Exuma,** I was the belle of the ball at one local hotspot. As soon as I'd come off the dance floor, there'd be yet another guy waiting to dance with me. One of these guys, with a gleam in his eyes, whispered to me, "My secret fantasy is to make it with a big woman."

In a LOUD voice, I asked, "Why is that a secret?"

"Be quiet, be quiet!" he growled at me.

I was stumped and gave him a "duh?" look. Why—on an island teeming with big women, and with men who obviously liked them that way—was he so embarrassed about wanting one himself? In the end, I flipped my hair over my shoulder, glared at him, and sauntered away. Who needed a gutless—and not very attractive—worm like him?

Not me. On that same night in Georgetown, the suave and very cute owner of a local restaurant and bar was all over me. As I made my way back to the restroom at one point, a couple of locals managed to inform me that he was married. When I got back to my table and he started to get touchy-feely again, I pushed him away. "No, you're married!" I said.

"But I'll get a divorce for you!" he said.

Next!

Later—yes, we're still on that *same* night—a tourist from Scotland spent a couple of hours holding my hand and gazing soulfully into my eyes. He suggested we go for a walk. I didn't want to leave the party . . . so he gave me a long, passionate kiss in full view of the other revelers.

Ah, those idyllic isles!

LATIN LOVERS

Forget Paris—the French are so petite. The same with Belgium—I've found Belgians to be typically tiny, too. But ooh-la-la! Those Latin lovers are hot, hot, hot . . . for *us*. I know plus-size girls who've been chased down the streets of Barcelona and Madrid. And as for Italy . . . well, even my mother—age sixty-something—gets her behind pinched there!

Let's talk about the many countries where curves are compulsory; where the Latin-based languages are referred to by linguists as the "romance" languages (how appropriate!). But you *don't* have to worry about language barriers. I discovered this first in **Peru.** I had scoped out an obvious surfer on my flight to Cuzco (the town closest to Machu Picchu) and, by sheer luck, later ran into him at a cafe. I used the little Spanish I knew to discover that he and his friend were Brazilians taking a tourist break from their "surfari" through Peru. He spoke only Portuguese, so our verbal communication was definitely limited. Nevertheless, we spent two fantastic days romancing and touring together—all we needed was the language of love.

Speaking of **Brazil** and Brazilians, my friend Leila, who is a transplanted Brazilian now living in San Clemente, says that in her native country, "You're considered beautiful if you have a bigger butt."

Big butts are also worshipped in **Spain** and **Portugal**, my former Manhattan roommate Kelly Repassy told *Mode*. So much so that she found herself wearing tighter, more revealing clothes than she ever dares to in the States. "My backside was so adored in Portugal that I thought about moving there after only three days," says Kelly, a plus-size model. "It was amazing to be seen as the ideal woman instead of the black sheep."

Italy and **Greece:** Greek isn't one of the romance languages, but Italian and Greek men are so similar in their tastes in women and their way of romancing that I'm speaking of them together. In my experience, Greek and Italian men love women, period. And it seems the more of a woman you are, the more of a turn-on you are. Stefano Silvestrini, a transplanted Italian who now lives in New York, told me that in his country, "Sophia Loren is still the ideal woman, and she is zaftig." As for Stefano's own personal tastes, "I don't care what a woman weighs. To me, sexiness is on the inside."

One of my favorite Italian restaurateurs—let's call him T.T.—told me that when he was growing up in Italy, women who were too thin were considered unhealthy and were suspected of being unable to breastfeed—which could hamper their chances on the marriage market. T.T. grew up on Italy's Adriatic coast, and he says when large German women tourists came there on vacation, the locals admiringly—not disparagingly—called them Amazons. "We like our women chubby," he says. "They're easier to grab onto!"

Lang Phipps, a writer who cheerfully admitted in *Mode* that since the age of fifteen he's "hungered for . . . warm, general roundness" in women, went on to write that on a recent trip to Italy he was delighted to witness "Italian stud types in the courting ritual with pretty but pudgy girls."

Greece is pretty much the same. A few years ago, in the Minneapolis airport, I met a Greek man who had moved from Athens to the United States when he was still a teen. He told me that when he arrived in the U.S. he was "completely turned off by the skinny backsides of American girls." He'd grown up admiring the "charming chubby cheeks" of his Greek female counterparts. These days, he says, he's grown more tolerant of the thinner American version of female perfection. "But I still hate a boney butt," he says, "and I'm so tired of sick-looking models who look like they've just been released from a concentration camp. Who wants to meet someone out of the grave? Not me!" He also proudly asserted—urging me to "Write this down!"— that Greeks have the reputation of being the best lovers in Europe!

In Greece and Italy, food is meant to be enjoyed, and women are actually urged to eat, eat, eat! Every meal is something of a celebration. If you take a pass on the pasta or fret about the fat in the feta, who wants you around?

Closer to home: When talk show host Rosie O'Donnell visited **Mexico** with a friend, she was shocked when "hordes of hombres" flocked to her side but barely glanced at her skinny model friend. "Every Mexican guy was hitting on me," Rosie later said in an HBO special. She was stumped about what was going on until one of her pursuers finally spilled his guts: "Bone is for the dog," he explained seductively, "meat is for the man." Speaking of talk show hosts and beef, Geraldo Rivera purportedly likes women with "meat on their bones," and he attributes it to growing up in a Latin culture.

My actor friend Gilbert, who is Mexican-American, theorizes that this charming trait in Latin men probably starts with their families. "Big women are all Mexican men know," Gilbert says. "They've grown up with moms who were big and they love their moms. Mexican girls just get big. It has come to a point where Mexican men don't even think about it; they just love a woman from the inside and accept her as she is on the outside. My uncles like larger women and they're happy. They tell me, 'Oh, I've had the skinny girl, and it's just not the same. I like my girls big.'"

GERMANY

Along with the U.S., Germany is a top market for plus-size models, proving that there are many big women there. German advertisers always depict plus-size models as sexy, whereas in the U.S. the "feel" of the photos is motherly.

AFRICA

Like Australia, this is a continent that has intrigued me since I was a child. I am counting on visiting it someday soon.

Says Catherine Lippincott in her book *Well Rounded: Eight Simple Steps to Changing Your Life, Not Your Size:* "I recently received a letter from a friend of mine (a beautiful red-headed size 18) who is living abroad. She writes: 'Did you know that in **Morocco** large-size women are called "forte," meaning "strong"? . . . A voluptuous woman (in Morocco) represents comfort, well-being, and a joy to her family.'"

I was unable to find any other plus-size women who have visited Africa, but I did glean some insight from a very thin black woman from **South Africa** who works in the plus-size department at Saks Fifth Avenue in L.A. She told me that when she was growing up in her country, she battled societal stigmas just like we do—except from the opposite point of view. Her father told her that she was too skinny and that she'd have to gain weight if she ever hoped to find a husband. Maybe that's why she came to America!

ASIA

According to my friend Liria Mersini, a designer, larger women may be far less common in Asia than they are in other parts of the world, but "thanks to an enduring history of religious reverence, there is an appreciative respect for people of size," she wrote in *BBW*. For example, **Hong Kong** has the world's largest outdoor bronze statue of Buddha at the Po Lin Monastery on Lantau Island. "Standing beneath this 100-foot-high, 200-ton big, beautiful person is truly awesome," she says.

She reports that her friend Andrea D'Angelo-Risner, who wears a size 22, was the center of attention at a hot night club in **Beijing**, where she danced the night away with the locals. My friend Martin, who has traveled throughout **China** and **Vietnam** as a photographer since the Vietnam War, tells me that big women are adored in those countries. Most of the population is poor, he says, and being big is seen as good fortune.

Liria also wrote that New York–based travel agent Rita Block Chouinard—who is plus-size herself—has one big female client who was continuously touched admiringly by the natives in **Bangkok**.

Think of the classic belly dancers of **India**, with their rounded tummies and ample, vibrating hips. Reverence for the ample female figures goes back to the beginning of Indian civilization. Zia Jaffrey, author of *The Invisibles*, a study of Indian culture, told *Mode* that "The erotic sculptures on temples depict women who are pleasingly plump and have prominent bellies and large breasts. Flesh is part of ideal femininity," she notes. Zia adds that in the *Kama Sutra*, that classic Indian text about love and lovemaking, women who walk with the gait of an elephant are considered especially beautiful. (I think I'll stick with my regular gait, though. I don't think my clients would appreciate my lumbering down a runway!)

THE AMERICAN SOUTH AND MIDWEST

If you live in either of these regions of the United States, you're probably wondering what the heck they're doing here in a chapter about other countries. Well, for those of us who live in New York or southern California, where staying thin is a religion, these regions *do* feel like foreign countries. It's quite refreshing—even empowering—to step off a plane in, say, Indianapolis or Savannah, and see that most women are *real* women, not the emaciated paper dolls you see at home.

Browsing through *Allure* magazine at my hair salon a few months ago, I came across some interesting statistics. The state with the most overweight (that word always makes me wonder, "Over *whose* weight?") people per capita is **Mississippi**, where 32 percent of the population is overweight. The American city with the most overweight people per capita? **New Orleans**, where 37.6 percent of the population tips the scales. I asked my friend Eleni, a native of New Orleans and a big woman who now lives in L.A., if she could explain her hometown's ranking. "First of all," Eleni says, "the food in New Orleans is probably the best food in the country. The nature of dining in New Orleans is to overeat. I have had meals all over Europe and the U.S., and the places that people claim have the best food—San Francisco is a good example—do not even come close. New Orleans is the capital of good food, and you get everything in huge portions."

Eleni continues: "Men in New Orleans tend to be a little bawdier, heartier, and more outgoing than men elsewhere, so typically I felt very comfortable around men there. I didn't feel like size was an issue. Obviously, wherever you go in the world, there will be a certain population of men whose perfect woman is 36-24-36, but in New Orleans, as a rule, I never felt uncomfortable, whether it was going to school or walking into a restaurant or bar. Nobody ever picked me out from the crowd and made fun of me because of my size."

She says she didn't experience that until she moved to L.A. "And that's because L.A. is a plastic, kind of on-the-surface town, where looks are pretty much your life, especially if you work in the entertainment industry, like I do."

An added bonus to life in New Orleans, according to Eleni: "The men there are very direct. They will let you know it if they're interested in you. What happens at Mardi Gras is the perfect example. There's a tradition during the festival: If you show your breasts, men present you with beads, and the bigger your breasts, the bigger the beads you get. Wearing those beads is a status symbol for women during Mardi Gras. And, believe me, when the men go to ask women for a little peek of their mammary glands, they go for the bigger women in the crowd. A sexist tradition? Exploitive? Well, think what you want, but the bottom line is it's an advantage to be a large woman in New Orleans."

KATIE'S BEST TRAVEL TIPS

1. **Figure out how much time and money you can spend, *then* choose your destination.** If you haven't traveled much before, I recommend limiting your first adven-

ture to an English-speaking country or countries. It helps to be able to speak with everyone and to read all the signs. Australia, New Zealand, and England are just a few of the many countries in which English is the first language. If you're a bit more brave your first time out, opt for a country—especially in Europe—where English is the second language. These countries are easy to get around in because nearly everybody speaks some English, and officials who can help you—such as police, hotel desk clerks, train reservation agents—often speak English fluently.

2. **After you've decided on your dream destination, hit the bookstores and the Internet, call the consulates, gather all the information you can.** Part of the excitement of taking a trip is in the anticipation. I always read about the country's history, as well as what to see and where to go. There are travel books for every destination in the world, and they're filled with everything you need to know about where to stay, how to get around, and how much money you can expect to spend. And the consulates will have up-to-date information on events and special offers you can take advantage of during the time you plan to visit. The consulates and travel books can also clue you in to local holidays that can screw up your plans. Last summer my coauthor and her boyfriend arrived for a one-day stay in Milan only to find that that day was a major religious holiday *only* in Milan. The entire city was closed down—all the shops, all the historical sites, all the restaurants. Except McDonald's, where the pair had to eat all three of their meals that day.

I advise you to collect information from these sources before making any flight or hotel arrangements, because often you will find money-saving tips that you won't learn about from your travel agent. Most travel agents sell the whole world, and it's hard for them to keep up on all the little details about every country. Let me give you an example: For one of my first trips to Australia, I carefully planned my itinerary with the help of a travel agent. I reserved a rental car and planned to spend two weeks slowly driving up the coast from Sydney to Brisbane. However, once I got there, I discovered that the "coastal" road was actually about an hour inland from the ocean. Booooring! I also discovered that the local airfare was much cheaper than the rental car. I canceled my hotels, drove straight to Brisbane, turned in the car, and bought a roundtrip airfare to Cairns. All for the same amount of money. Which leads right into my third tip . . .

3. **Make your plans loosely.** Open returns aren't that much more expensive and they add extra spontaneity to your adventure. At home, we all live on a schedule: Up at 7, to work by 8:30, lunch from 12 to 12:45, etc. When you travel, take a vacation from schedules! These days I make hotel arrangements only for the first few nights, then wing it once I get there. Yes, I've had a couple of close calls, such as arriving to find no vacant hotel rooms. Luckily, though, it always seems to work out okay.

4. **Get off the "tourist path" so you can meet the real people of the country.** Often when people travel they spend all of their time doing all of the typical tourist things. When you do that you meet only other tourists . . . or locals who work with tourists. There's nothing wrong with that—I've made some great friends of fellow travelers—but you won't get the real flavor of the country, its people, and its culture. Instead, wander on your own to small towns, ask locals where they go out to dinner or to view the sunset, or to unwind. When you get off the beaten path, you will find locals who generally don't meet tourists,

and so are eager to meet you. Many times they will offer to show you around, or even invite you home for dinner. And by meeting the locals you'll discover that—no matter what the environment, culture, or language—we are all pretty much alike (EXCEPT for the all-American obsession with being thin!).

I know many, many women who seem to have no trouble getting men. And they are not beauty queens; they come in all sizes—including *our* sizes. Some might say it's because they're easy, that the guys just use them for sex and move on. But with most of these women I know, the men call again and again—and not just for sex, but for dinner, dancing, and even lifelong relationships. These girls are heartbreakers. What's their secret? Easy. They're sexy and confident.

So how do you get sexy? Start with this: Actress Uma Thurman once said that "vanity is sexy"; that is, if you believe that you are sexy and beautiful, and you let people know it, they will see you that way.

Here's another secret: The more confident you are in your lovemaking abilities, the more you will exude a sexy image. All my life I've read how important it is to feel totally comfortable with your body in order to enjoy good sex. I always denied this and felt that I had a great sex life even though I hated my body. It wasn't until years later, when I began to like my body, that I realized that it is true: SEX IS BETTER WHEN YOU'RE TOTALLY AT PEACE WITH YOUR BODY! As I've said before, it takes a lot of work and time to truly become comfortable with your body, but anyone can do it. Here's how:

REMEMBER THIS: BIGGER WOMEN ARE SEXIER THAN THINNER WOMEN!

No, this is not some affirmation I made up for you to repeat when you're feeling down. Scientists came up with this finding in a bona fide study. In her book *Fat and Thin*, Anne Scott Beller states that "fat women are more sexually appetitive than thin women are." These results stunned the researchers at Michael Reese Hospital in Chicago, who conducted the study and who figured that the results would turn out to be exactly the opposite. They had started out with that tired old theory that fat women become fat and stay that way "largely as a means of insulating themselves from the give and take of mature, heterosexual relationships," as *Fat and Thin* put it. The researchers thought that ". . . the fatter a woman was, the less likely she would be to have an active and satisfactory sex life—on the one hand because her partners could be expected to find her unappetizing to begin with, and on the other hand because the same defense mechanisms that were supposed to have led her to get fat in the first place should by the same token have operated to make her frigid in the second." (What morons!)

But that assumption was proved wrong. The amazed (and dim-witted) researchers found that the fatter women in the study were significantly "sexier" than the thinner subjects. Reports *Fat and Thin*, "In terms of erotic readiness and general excitability, fat women outscored their thin sisters by a factor of almost two to one." You go, girls! All of the women in the survey—fat and thin—were married, and all reported roughly the same amount of regular sexual intercourse (about nine times a month). But an overwhelming majority of the fat women stated that they would have liked to have sex more often, while a significant number of the thinner subjects were perfectly content with their frequency of intercourse. The researchers concluded that "these women obviously weren't overeating instead of having sex; their craving for both sex and food exists almost simultaneously."

Hooray for large appetites!

GYM BENEFITS

Big, big talent Aretha Franklin recently told *Mode* magazine that she walks and jogs three miles a day to stay in shape. "But you know what the best way is?" asks Aretha. *"Young men!"*

Are young men in short supply in your life? That's when the gym comes in handy. Aside from its health benefits, exercise is important because it keeps you strong. One of the main things that makes big women attractive to men is our strength. Be strong, and don't be afraid to flaunt that strength when you are making love.

Back to the gym: Stretch first. It will loosen you up and make you limber—a great attribute in the bedroom! Concentrate your workout on the lower half of your body. In the weight room (a visit there is a must), use the inner and outer thigh machines. Toning those thigh muscles stimulates our sex muscles! One of my best friends swears by the Thighmaster. She has amazing legs and she is always rarin' to go. Let's face it: Working out increases your sex drive. It makes you horny, honey, and there's nothing wrong with that!

INNER GYMNASTICS

As I've said throughout this book, we must educate ourselves, specifically for *our* needs. The more knowledge you have about what turns you on sexually, the more confident you'll be while making love. There are many, many books of advice on how to have steamy sex. I've borrowed and read only a few—some of the tips in the books were absurd, others hokey, still others very educational. I put some of what I learned to the test. The effectiveness? It varied. Some guys, for example, get turned on by a hand rubbed up the back of the thigh. For other guys, this is about as arousing as a test of the Emergency Broadcast System. I won't detail all the other tricks I have experimented with—this isn't one of those books!

But! . . . I will share this winning bit of advice: Exercise your private parts through isometrics. Since I read that, I've learned that these exercises are called Kegels (named after Arnold Kegel, the gynecologist who invented them). If you've ever had a baby, you may already know about Kegels, since many ob/gyns recommend that women do them after birth to tighten the vagina.

Kegels are squeezes of the perineal muscles. You can learn which muscles to squeeze by stopping your urine midflow. What's the beauty of Kegels? You can do them anywhere, any time, and no one's the wiser. I've even done them in front of the camera.

Get in the habit of squeezing off a hundred Kegels a day. Do them every day while you're driving to work, or when you're loading the dishwasher, or when you're watching your favorite sitcom.

Kegels will not only make intercourse feel better for you, your lover will notice the difference, as well. In fact, for a real thrill, do some Kegels while your partner is inside you. Men *adore* this!

ALL BY YOURSELF

Don't be ashamed—masturbate! This will help you discover what feels good, and you can pass that knowledge along to your lover. Buy a toy! If you're too embarrassed to go to a sex shop, get one of those catalogs advertised in the back pages of magazines like *Cosmopolitan.* Find your own sexuality. When your sexual organs are stimulated, they become more sensitive, which makes sex better for you. And when you're more into the experience, believe me, so is your partner.

You can also learn a lot about sex from porn videos, but try to choose one produced by one of the many houses now specializing in porn that's directed to a female viewer. How to find such videos? The companies that produce these videos have feminine names like Tigress and Blush.

Fantasize! Draw yourself a candlelit bath and pour a glass of wine. Take the events of a particular day and create a great fantasy around them. For example, think about the sexy guy in your office who smiled at you today, and who calls to say he's just filed for divorce, and can he come over? That's just the beginning . . . (Incidentally, I also use that particular fantasy as motivation to clean up my house!)

One caution: Keep your fantasies for your own pleasure, and don't let them take over your life. In other words, don't opt for your bath over a night out with the girls.

ENTERTAINING: STIMULATE ALL OF HIS SENSES

Sight, sound, smell, taste, touch—all affect our mood. Imagine inviting a man over for dinner without giving any thought to the senses in advance. He knocks on the door, the door opens and exudes a great whiff of garlic, and the person who opens the door—you—is just a dark silhouette with a bright light glowing around her, making him squint. He assumes it's you and comes inside even though he can't see you or hear you over the blaring music. After he realizes it's you, he gives you a hug, only to scratch his face on the polyester collar of your blouse. All of this is a sensual disaster! Experiment with sight, sound, smell, taste, and touch. Find your preferences; those that are pleasing to your senses will please his, too.

Lighting. I learned the importance of lighting from modeling. When I first started, I read a few books on modeling and they all said to "work the light." It took me a while to figure out that working the light to your best advantage also means working the shadows. A hip pointed toward the light puts a shadow on the other hip, making you look slimmer. A bright light from above your face can make you look drawn and gives you circles under your eyes. On the other hand, a bright light from below can make your face look ghostly and spooky and accentuates a double chin. It's important to find the happy medium whenever you have control over the lighting.

I have spent many nights experimenting with the lighting in my apartment. I use different-color lightbulbs and candles. One look is great for entertaining a crowd that will be dancing. Another is just right for a dinner party. And a third is perfect for an intimate evening for two! Lighting is important: It sets the mood.

When you're outside, work the sunlight. Looking into the sun can make your eyes sparkle and shine. I'm not talking about harsh, noontime sun that will make you squint and can harm your eyes. I mean early-morning sun, and the golden sun of the late afternoon, and—especially—sunset.

Scents. Another secret is to have incense burning. Being extrasensitive to smell, I tried hundreds of different kinds of incense before I found the one that became my signature scent. Just don't overwhelm your guest with it. Burn the incense before he arrives, or place it in a back corner of the room. You want just a hint of it and, more important,

How to Make Love to a Man—Big Time 155

you want him to be able to smell *you* when he is nuzzling your neck, not "Sweet Rain."

Scented candles are an alternative to incense.

The Sound of Music. Unless your evening's planned activity is to watch the television, never, ever have the TV on when you're entertaining. It's distracting, and you don't want distractions. And yet silence can be uncomfortable. The solution is background music. If you're dating a drummer, play it loud! Otherwise, keep it at a nice, soft volume that you can comfortably speak over. Plan in advance: Select music appropriate for the evening—you know, Mozart over the filet mignon and old Barry White make-out music for later!

Touch. When you know your man is going to spend the evening hugging you, give him a soft sensation. Make sure your skin is freshly shaven and moisturized, and wear soft and sexy fabrics like silk, satin, cashmere, or velvet instead of scratchy and/or rough material like polyester and wool.

Also, what is your couch made of? Is it stiff and noisy Naugahyde? If so, consider buying a new couch, or at least drape the one you have with a throw blanket in preparation for intimate moments. Nobody likes sticking to Naugahyde.

If you think that the evening's plans might take you into the bedroom, make that room as romantic and sensual as possible. Remember the draped walls and pillow-filled beds the ancient Egyptians had in those old DeMille extravaganzas? Re-create that mood. I have a sheer curtain next to my bed that divides my bedroom into a bedroom and a dressing room. It works great! I can stand naked behind my sheer curtain and dress in front of my man without him seeing every dented detail of my curves! And my bedding is soft cotton with a velvet cover. Even alone I feel like a queen.

TAKE CONTROL

Okay, you've got the guy, you're on the couch kissing, and he starts to move his hands to caress you. You start thinking about that tummy bulge he's about to discover. Or maybe it's that roll at the back of your waist. Or maybe he's getting awfully close to those dimples on the back of your thigh. *Oh, my God—what will he think? Will he be turned off?*

How can you enjoy yourself with these kinds of thoughts racing through your mind? Until you gain complete and ultimate confidence in yourself and truly love every dent and bulge on your body, you won't be able to enjoy his caressing. But I assure you, this *can* happen. Especially if he helps. One of my ex-boyfriends loved my softness. I couldn't stop him from going to my most fat-sensitive areas. He would grab me by the fat and scream with pleasure. He loved it!

Other boyfriends, though, have been less, shall we say, "chubby friendly." I have been the first chubbette for many of them, and I could tell they weren't used to the softness. Whenever this happens, though, I take control: If his caresses are heading for one of those extrasoft areas, I simply take his hand and move it to another pleasure zone, preventing any discomfort for either of us. Guys don't know the true reasoning behind such a move—they just feel they're getting closer to the action!

UNDERCOVER

In an earlier chapter I talked about the importance of good undergarments. But what do you do with those so-called shapers at the end of the night when the petting begins? This very situation was depicted quite realistically in the movie *St. Elmo's Fire* (rent it) when Mare Winningham's character finally gets a chance to get physical with her crush, the infamous Rob Lowe. They start to kiss, and as Rob rubs his hand up her thigh, he discovers her girdle and makes fun of it. She gets upset and the session is over.

Avoid this disaster. Simply excuse yourself after the kissing starts, go to the bathroom, and get that girdle off! Make sure that you always carry a large enough purse in which to stash such a garment. Then, go back to your guy pantyless. He'll be happily surprised! He'll wonder if you've gone all night without panties—and, ooh, if he thinks you did, what a naughty girl you are! Men love that stuff!

And what if you don't want to go there? Okay, be cool and in control and don't let him know that you are pantyless. He can touch your thigh without feeling that modern chastity belt called a girdle, shapewear, whatever. Just stop his hand before he discovers that you're "sitting free"!

POSITIONS, PLEASE!

One fear that probably crosses your mind while making love with someone is . . . *What do I look like right now? What does he see?* When you're self-conscious about your body, you get into the habit of insisting on the missionary position. And why not? Lying on your back is comfortable, and gravity pulls everything away from his view. Sure, to get on top, to bounce up and down, to *move* more can certainly be more fun—but then he'll see you shake and jiggle, right? Any woman with large breasts knows that aside from what it looks like, it's uncomfortable to flop around. There's a simple solution: Wear a bra. A lacy, plunging, sexy bra can be an incredible turn-on for a man, and you'll be more comfortable to boot. Is it your tummy you're worried about? Why not have sex with your dress on—or perhaps leave open your very sexy blouse.

If you're uneasy about his caressing while you're on top, grab his hands and hold them down. He's been a bad boy and you're in control! You-on-top is one of the positions in which you can exert your strength. Use those inner thigh muscles to move him from side to side. With practice, you can even lift him closer to you with your thighs.

It's fun to be in control, but don't go overboard, okay? Give him have plenty of chances to be in charge. Enjoy being at his command, too.

BE ADVENTUROUS

A wild and crazy girl can be a huge turn-on for a guy. Example: The first time I went swimming naked (I hate the term "skinny dipping"), it was night and I was petrified. No, not because I was on an island in the middle of the shark-infested Great Barrier Reef. I was scared because the moon was out, and the others could see me in my birthday suit. Once I got in the water, however, and felt the cool sensation of being at one with Mother Nature, all my fears disappeared. Soon, I was confident enough to dive into the black sea. There was a slide on a platform twenty yards off the coast, and I will never in my life forget the bracing shock of flying through the air not knowing when I would hit the ocean. The exuberant freedom I expressed with my body was a total turn-on to the man my sight was set on. He told me so later as he walked me back to my cabin and kissed me goodnight. We spent the following two weeks together traveling through northern Queensland. Another amazing experience that almost never was because of my insecurity about my body.

You don't have to be halfway around the world in some

exotic locale to be adventurous. I am sure there's a romantic hideaway right in your hometown. There's something special about making love under the stars. Maybe it's the potential danger that someone may see you, or maybe it's just the connection to nature. Either way—explore your world and find your favorite romantic spot.

My friend Robin and I each have our own special cliffside in my hometown. Mine is better—a tree hides me from the nearest home, and the view of the ocean and the coastal lights is breathtaking. It's not only my romantic spot; it's my own personal meditation spot. I've experienced many sunsets, fits of tears, and bursts of inspiration from that cliff. It's my sacred place, and only special men have accompanied me there.

I will never forget that birthday of mine when my guy stood naked with the wind blowing his long hair. He was silhouetted by stars and the moon's reflection on the ocean while I sang "Happy Birthday to Me!"

ORGANIZATIONS

About Face, P.O. Box 77665, San Francisco, CA 94107; (415) 436-0212; Web site: http://www.about-face.org. Fosters self-esteem for women.

Abundia, P.O. Box 252, Downers Grove, IL 60575; (708)963-0346. Programs for the promotion of body-size acceptance and self-esteem.

AHELP, the Association for the Health Enrichment of Large People, P.O. Box 11743, Blackburg, VA 24062; (540) 552-0067; fax: (540) 951-3527.

Ample Opportunity, P.O. Box 40621, Portland, OR 97240; (503) 245-1524.

The Association for Full-Figured Women, P.O. Box 371926, Decatur, GA 30037; (404)243-6862.

Big Options, 9220 A-1 Parkway East, Suite 127, Birmingham, AL 35206; (205) 854-6399; fax: (205) 856-4535; email: loraw@hotmail.com. An information-based effort to educate society on what's available for large people. Free resource guides.

Body Image Task Force, P.O. Box 934, Santa Cruz, CA 96061; (408) 426-1821. Promotes consciousness raising on the issues of lookism and fatphobia. Distributes brochures, articles, and videos to help consumers make informed decisions about health care and how to assert their rights.

Council on Size & Weight Discrimination, Inc., P.O. Box 305, Mount Marion, NY 12456; (914) 679-1209; fax: (914) 679-1206. The council's mission is to influence public opinion and policy in order to end oppression based on discriminatory standards of body size, shape, or weight.

Diet/Weight Liberation, Annabel Taylor Hall, Cornell University, Ithaca, NY 14853; (607) 257-0563. A nonprofit self-help group that sponsors "Fed Up" groups and trains high school girls to present size-acceptance workshops to their peers.

International No-Diet Coalition, P.O. Box 305, Mt. Marion, NY 12456; (914) 679-1209. Send $1 and SASE for materials.

Largely Positive, P.O. Box 17223, Glendale, WI 53217. A support group for overweight women and men.

Largesse, 74 Woolsey Street, New Haven, CT 06513; (203) 787-1624 (phone/fax). A resource network for size esteem.

Media Action Alliance, P.O. Box 391, Circle Pines, MN 55014; (612) 434-4343. Challenges exploitation and violence against women.

Vitality, formerly PLEASE (Promoting Lifelong Education About Self-Esteem), 91 South Main St., West Hartford, CT 06107; (860) 521-2515; fax: (860) 521-8291.

NAAFA, National Association to Advance Fat Acceptance, P.O. Box 188620, Sacramento, CA 95818; (800) 442-1214. A nonprofit human rights organization dedicated to improving the quality of life for fat people through public education, research, advocacy, and member support.

PUBLICATIONS

Belle, P.O. Box 419, Mt. Morris, IL 61054; (800) 877-5549. A magazine for the full-figured African-American woman.

Canada Wyde, P.O. Box 511-99, Dalhousie Street, Toronto, Ontario, Canada M5B2N2; (416) 861-0217. A quarterly magazine for large Canadians and their admirers.

Dimensions, P.O. Box 640, Folsom, CA 95763; (916) 984-9947. A bimonthly magazine for men who prefer big women, but also has many good articles by and for women. Features hundreds of personal ads from big women and their admirers.

Extra Hip, 6201 Sunset Boulevard, #94, Hollywood, CA 90028; (213) 461-9506; fax: (213) 464-3908; e-mail: Xhip@aol.com. This is the quarterly newsletter published by Katie Arons for fashion-conscious plus-size teenage and young women. Free subscription.

FAT! So?, P.O. Box 423-464, San Francisco, CA 94142. A quarterly 'zine for people who don't apologize for their size.

HUES, New Moon Publishing, P.O. Box 3587, Duluth, MN 55803; (800) 483-7482. Size-positive, multicultural, upbeat, funny magazine that promotes good body image and self-esteem. Targeted at women age seventeen through college.

MODE, P.O. Box 54275, Boulder, CO 80323; (888) 610-6633. A fashion/beauty magazine for women who wear size 12 and over.

New Moon, P.O. Box 3587, Duluth, MN 55803; (218) 728-5507. The little sister of *HUES*, this magazine deals with issues of importance to eight- to fourteen-year-old girls, including a positive body image and self-esteem.

Radiance, P.O. Box 30246, Oakland, CA 94604; (510) 482-0680. Often features successful large women, articles encouraging size acceptance, and a little bit of feminism, fashion, poetry, and other size-positive expressions.

Rump Parliament, P.O. Box 181716, Dallas, TX 75218. A magazine working to change the way society treats fat people. It is a forum for discussion of the many forms of antidiet size acceptance and rights activism.

BOOKS

Historical and Contemporary Looks at Women's Body Image

American Beauty, by historian Lois W. Banner (Alfred A. Knopf, 1983). A social history through two centuries of the American idea, ideal, and image of the beautiful woman.

The Beauty Myth, by Naomi Wolf (Anchor Books, 1992). An eye-opening exposé of our society's beauty standards, including an extensive analysis of hunger, dieting, and weight issues.

Fat & Thin, by anthropologist Anne Scott Beller (Farrar, Straus, and Giroux, 1978). A natural history of obesity through the centuries.

Such a Pretty Face: Being Fat in America, by sociologist Marcia Millman (W.W. Norton & Co., 1986).

Exploding Fat Fallacies
Are You Too Fat, Ginny?, by Karin Jasper (Is Five, 1988). Targeted at young girls, this book challenges myths about fatness and dieting in adolescents and fosters size acceptance.

Big Fat Lies: The Truth About Your Weight and Your Health, by Glenn Gaesser, Ph.D. (Fawcett Books, 1996; Ballantine, 1998). A synthesis of the latest medical literature that challenges common beliefs about weight, e.g., you can't be fat and fit.

Breaking All the Rules, by Nancy Roberts (Penguin Books, 1978). "Be concerned," says the author, "that you're eating a healthy diet, getting all your vitamins and minerals, and stop worrying. Some people are just big, and society has to accept that."

Fat Is Not a Four-Letter Word, by Charles Roy Schroeder (Chronimed, 1992). Shatters stereotypes and debunks myths about being fat plus provides a powerful exposé of the diet industry.

The Forbidden Body: Why Being Fat Is Not a Sin, by Shelley Bovey (Pandora Press, 1994). Puts tough questions to surgeons, dietitians, and doctors and helps women to lose guilt and inhibitions, not weight.

The Invisible Woman: Confronting Weight Prejudice in America, by W. Charisse Goodman (Gurze Books, 1995). A powerful, angry exposé of size discrimination and its connections to sexism, health, the mass media, food, power, and other prejudice.

Rethinking Obesity: An Alternative View of Its Health Implications, by Paul Ernsberger and Paul Haskew (Human Sciences Press, 1987). A rebuttal to the old NIH panel pronouncement that obesity is a "killer disease."

Dieting/Nondieting

Diet-Breaking: Having It All Without Having to Diet, by Mary Evans Young (Hodder/Headline). How to end the guilt trip, begin to look and feel better about yourself, and break free of the diet trap forever.

The Dieter's Dilemma, by William Bennett and Joel Gurin (Basic Books, 1982). The set-point theory and why diets don't work.

Fed Up! A Woman's Guide to Freedom From the Diet Weight Prison, by Terry Nicholetti Garrison with David Levitsky (Carroll & Graf Books, 1993). These authors say that the weight-loss industry is selling products that don't work while convincing consumers that it's their fault.

Health Risks of Weight Loss, by Frances M. Berg (Healthy Weight Journal, 1995). The latest info on the health risks of weight loss.

Life Isn't Weighed on the Bathroom Scales, by Laura Rose (WRS, 1994). A passionate invitation to escape from dieting and embrace living.

Losing It: America's Obsession with Weight Loss, by Laura Fraser (Dutton, 1997). An investigative report on the science and economics driving the medical community and diet industry to play on our fears and talk us into buying ineffective and harmful pills, diets, surgery, and other gimmicks.

Stop Dieting—Start Living, by Sharon Greene Patton (Dodd, Mead & Co., 1985). How one angry woman finally gave up dieting, regained her self-esteem, and stopped feeling ashamed, guilty, rejected, and a failure.

Size Acceptance
Am I Fat?, by Joanne P. Ikeda and Priscilla Naworski (ETR Associates, 1993). Helping young children accept differences in body size.

Journeys to Self-Acceptance: Fat Women Speak, edited by Carol Wiley (Crossing Press, 1994). Twenty first-person accounts of women who have found their way out of weight-loss madness.

One Size Fits All and Other Fables, by Liz Curtis Higgs (Thomas Nelson, 1993). A wonderful, humorous introduction to size and self-acceptance.

Otherwise Perfect: People and Their Problems with Weight, by Mary S. Stuart and Lynnzy Orr (Health Communications, 1987).

Overcoming Fear of Fat, by Laura S. Brown and Esther Roth-
blum, Ph.D. (Harrington Park Press, 1989). Experts share
personal and professional experiences of challenging fat
oppression.

Shadow on a Tightrope: Writings by Women on Fat Oppression,
by Lisa Shoenfielder and Barb Wiesar (Aunt Lute Books,
1983). A collection of articles, personal stories, and poems
by fat women. It was the first book to present fat liberation
and its connection to feminism.

Improving Your Self-Esteem and/or Body Image
*Body Traps: Breaking the Binds That Keep You From Feeling
Good About Yourself*, by Judith Rodin, Ph.D. (Morrow,
1993). The author is a psychologist.

Come Out, Come Out, Wherever You Are, by Carole Shaw
(American R.R., 1982). The former editor of *BBW* magazine invites you to be beautiful and feel good about yourself
at any size.

*Live Large! Ideas, Affirmations, and Actions for Sane Living
in a Large Body*, by Cheri Erdman, Ed.D. (Harper-
Collins, 1997). Day-by-day, week-by-week ways in which
large women can learn to live with and celebrate their
bodies.

*Love Your Looks: How to Stop Criticizing and Start Appreciat-
ing Your Appearance*, by Carolynn Hillman (Simon &
Schuster, 1996). This compassionate guide shows you
how to get beyond societal or self-imposed standards
and learn to accept and appreciate your own special attractiveness.

Never Too Thin: Why Women Are At War with Their Bodies, by Roberta Pollack Seid (Prentice Hall, 1989). Recognizes the roots of our society's obsession with thinness and looks to a future where we can rid ourselves of weight obsession and regain control of our lives.

Nothing to Lose: A Guide to Sane Living in a Large Body, by Cheri Erdman, Ed.D. (Harper San Francisco, 1995). A resource for helping large women learn to live with their bodies. Her mantra: "We don't have a weight problem, society does."

Revolution From Within: A Book of Self-Esteem, by Gloria Steinem (Little, Brown, 1993). Even the gorgeous First Feminist had trouble learning to love herself.

Self-Esteem Comes in All Sizes, by Carol A. Johnson (Doubleday, 1995). How to be happy and healthy at your natural weight. The author is the founder of Largely Positive, a support group for overweight women and men.

Transforming Body Image: Learning to Love the Body You Have, by Marcia Germaine Hutchinson, Ed.D. (Crossing Press, 1988). This book provides twenty-two comprehensive exercises that show the reader how to use the power of imagination to recognize and change distorted bodily perceptions and attitudes.

Well Rounded: Eight Steps for Changing Your Life . . . Not Your Size, by Catherine Lippincott (Pocket Books, 1997). A good entry-level book for the newcomer to fat acceptance.

What Do You See When You Look in the Mirror?, by Thomas F. Cash, Ph.D. (Bantam Books, 1995). A reassuring manual from one of America's top body image researchers.

When Women Stop Hating Their Bodies, by Jane R. Hirschman and Carol A. Munter (Ballantine Books, 1995). Explores the myriad reasons women insist on dieting, despite overwhelming evidence that diets don't work. Also delves into compulsive eating and obsession with body size.

Worth Your Weight, by Barbara Altman Bruno, Ph.D. (Rutledge, 1996). This book empowers you to take charge of your own life and make the decisions that are right for you, allowing you to move toward a happier, healthier, and more satisfying life.

Health/Fitness/Style/Beauty
Delta Style: Eve Wasn't a Size 6 and Neither Am I, by Delta Burke and Alexis Lipsitz (St. Martin's Press, 1998). The actress has written a book that's part memoir, part personal photo album, part beauty and fashion advice manual, and part resource guide for where to get large-sized clothing.

Great Shape, by Pat Lyons and Debby Burgard (Bull Publishing, 1990). An exercise guide for large women with emphasis on health and fun, rather than weight loss.

The H-O-A-X Fashion Formula: Dress the Body Type You Have to Look Like the Body You Want, by Mary Duffy, Gabrielle Bostrom, and Michael Markiw (The Body Press, 1987).

Read more about this fantastic book in the chapter "The Outer Shell."

Image Impact: The Complete Makeover Guide, edited by Jacqueline Thompson (Bristol Books, 1990). This book really helped me find my own style.

Just the Weigh You Are, by Stephen Jonas, M.D. and Linda Konner (Chapters Publishing, 1997). How to be fit and healthy whatever your size.

Lucy's List: A Comprehensive Sourcebook for Making Large Living Easier, by Lucy D.L. Curtis (Warner Books, 1996). Includes where to find clothes, uniforms, shoes, health-care items, furniture, appliances, and more.

Plus Style: The Plus-Size Guide to Looking Great, by Suzan Nanfeldt (Plume/Penguin, 1996).

Size Wise, by Judy Sullivan (Avon, 1997). A catalog of more than 1,000 resources for living with confidence and comfort at any size.

Style Is Not a Size, by Hara Estroff Marano (Bantam, 1991). Looking and feeling great in the body you have.

The Ultimate Plus-Size Modeling Guide, by Catherine Schuller (E.V.E., self-published, 1996, 800/759-7747). Want to be a model?

Thin Is Just a Four-Letter Word, by Dee Hakala with Michael D'Orso (Little, Brown, 1997). Living fit for all shapes and sizes. A valuable resource for anyone who's felt left out of the fitness revolution.

True Beauty Emme, by Emme with Daniel Paisner (Putnam, 1997). Positive attitudes and practical tips from the world's leading plus-size model.

Goddesses (see the chapter "How to Feel as Special as You Are)

The New Book of Goddesses and Heroines, by Patricia Monaghan (Llewellyn Publications, 1997).

The Once and Future Goddess, by Elinor Gadon (Harper-Collins, 1989).

ON-LINE SUPPORT

The Ample Living Forum on CompuServe. To access: GO AMPLE. On-line support group for people of size. Message sections and libraries cover such topics as self-esteem, medical research, health, employment issues, and fashion. Sections also available for family and friends who want to offer support.

FAT! SO? Home page: http://www.fatso.com. As innovative, gutsy, and comforting as the printed version (see Publications).

Grand Style Women's Club. Web site: http://www.grand-style.com. Where size 14+ women can speak with experts, shop, learn more about fitness, entertaining, and how to locate hard-to-find products and services. I write their teen column.

NAAFA's Web site: http://naafa.org. The National Association to Advance Fat Acceptance is a nonprofit human rights organization dedicated to improving the life of fat people through public education, research, advocacy, and member support.